D0868451

THE NATURE OF
SCIENTIFIC
EXPLANATION

JUDE P. DOUGHERTY

THE NATURE OF
SCIENTIFIC
EXPLANATION

THE CATHOLIC UNIVERSITY OF
AMERICA PRESS
Washington, D.C.

Library of Congress Cataloging-in-Publication Data
Dougherty, Jude P., 1930–
The nature of scientific explanation / Jude P. Dougherty.
p. cm.
Includes bibliographical references (p.   ) and index.
ISBN 978-0-8132-2013-0 (cloth : alk. paper) —
ISBN 978-0-8132-2014-7 (pbk. : alk. paper)
1. Science—Philosophy.
2. Knowledge, Theory of.   I. Title.
Q175.3.D68 2013
501—dc23   2012023293

FOR

ROBERT SOKOLOWSKI

CONTENTS

PREFACE

This volume is based on a set of lectures delivered at the Charles University, Prague, in 1991, lectures subsequently expanded and delivered on several university campuses or before philosophical associations. I do not claim that any part of this book is especially profound or original. This does not mean that the topics discussed are insignificant. The book draws upon the work of many others who have made it possible for me to write. Some of the facts, observations, and ideas presented in these lectures may seem to the specialist in need of documentary corroboration. The author agrees but has decided to expose himself to the challenge of skeptical colleagues.

Admittedly it is difficult to write about science in the abstract. There are many sciences, each employing a methodology of its own appropriate to its object of study. The Latin term, *scientia,* means knowledge. But not all knowledge can claim to be scientific. Enumeration is not science, nor is technology to be equated with science, though it is often thought of as such. Precise observation is not science, nor is the correlation of data that at first blush seem to be related. We speak of medical science when we mean the art of medicine. Engineering, too, is thought of as science but, like medicine, engineering draws upon a wealth of scientifically achieved information, but is not itself a science. The systematic collection of data is often taken to be scientific, as is the ability to make prediction based on the accumulation of data with respect to past instances. The application of scientific information is essentially an art with its own rules of application, much like prudence is the application of wisdom. We may not think of theology as a science, but Aristotle made room for a "divine science." Today we call it "natural theology" and distinguish it from sacred theology—that is, theology that has as its premises propositions derived from revelation. There is a whole cadre of disciplines we categorize as social science, but most of the time when we talk about science we have in mind natural science. Few think of philosophy and theology as science, although the case can be made that both in their foremost representatives constitute scientific inquiry.

These lectures will argue from a realist perspective that the fundamental goal of science is to render intelligible that which is unintelligible in terms of itself. They will insist, contrary to popular opinion, that science is not reducible to description, to prediction, or to control, but rather is directed to an understanding of the processes of nature. It must be admitted that theories that purport to describe the nature of scientific explanation vary as widely as philosophies vary. A philosophy of science is but a part of one's overarching metaphysical outlook, itself painstakingly derived from considerations of nature, law, intelligibility, causality, and inference. Most philosophies of science have been shaped by the social and intellectual milieu in which they arise. Our discussion of these will take notice of the historical situation in which they were initially offered, for the history of philosophy is much more a part of philosophy than the history of science is a part of physics.

These lectures are delivered from an Aristotelian point of view, employing the texts of Aristotle as commented upon and amplified over the centuries. Although challenged by modernity, that point of view remains viable. As we will subsequently show, modernity cannot be understood apart from its break with Plato and Aristotle. The fortunes of Aristotle are bound up with the fortunes of metaphysics. Once the core of any philosophical curriculum, metaphysics has become, where it is still pursued, one specialized discipline among many. In the golden age of American philosophy—the age of Peirce, James, Royce, Whitehead, and Santayana—and later even by the pragmatic naturalists who followed the lead of John Dewey, the centrality of metaphysics was uncontested. The eclipse of metaphysics is due in part to the ascendant influence of British analytic philosophy insofar as it reduces philosophy to logical and linguistic analysis. Some will speak of analytical metaphysics, but that upon scrutiny may turn out to be an oxymoron.

In the last decades of the twentieth century, pragmatic naturalists such as John Herman Randall, Jr., and Abraham Edel adapted Aristotle to suit their purpose, but remained philosophical realists. They did not subscribe to the analytic philosophy emanating from Oxford and Cambridge. Traditional metaphysical issues, including discussions of substance, causality, and purpose in nature—all of which have a bearing on how science is understood—were still pursued, albeit from a materialistic point of view. The materialism of Dewey and his school was motivated by an aversion to the so-called supernatural and the consequences it implied for the social and political order. Driven by skepticism with respect to the intellect's ability to causally reason from the seen to the unseen, Randall could produce a book on Aristotle omitting any reference to Aristotle's separated substance, an immaterial intellect, a prime mover, or a self-thinking intellect. In a bestselling textbook, Ernest Nagel, although employing the language of Aristotle, reduced scientific explanation to description and prediction. The implications were felt beyond the confines of the academy. It signaled a contest between factions for the direction of American education at all levels, the outcome of which has affected the subject matter of this volume.

In the early days of the American republic, philosophy was the province of the New England divines, those same ministers who laid the foundations of what were to become some of America's most prestigious universities. By the end of the eighteenth century it was recognized that British empiricism and Enlightenment philosophy, originating in France and Germany, were posing a threat to the Christian faith. *The Journal of Speculative Philosophy,* the first journal of philosophy in the English language, was established at St. Louis in 1867, among other reasons, to combat the secular philosophies arriving from Europe. The chosen mode of counterattack was that of German idealism, particularly the idealism of Hegel. In its first issue its editor, William Torrey Harris, explained the purpose of the journal. He gave three reasons. In his judgment speculative philosophy provides, first, a philosophy of religion much needed at a time when traditional religious teaching and ecclesiastical authority were losing their influence. Second, it provides a social philosophy compatible with a communal outlook, as opposed to a socially devastating individualism. Third, while taking cognizance of the startling advances in the natural sciences, it provides an alternative to empiricism as a philosophy of knowledge.

Speculative philosophy for Harris is a tradition that begins with Plato, a tradition that finds its full expression, he believed, in the system of Hegel.

The foremost representative of the speculative outlook endorsed by Harris was undoubtedly Josiah Royce, whose Gifford lectures (1900–1901), published as *The World and the Individual,* sought not only to counter the skepticism of the day, but to provide a rational foundation for the Christian faith. Royce had little respect for blind faith. The problem created by Kant's destruction of metaphysics he regarded as fundamental. In 1881 Royce wrote, "We all live, philosophically speaking, in a Kantian atmosphere." Eschewing the outright voluntarism of Schopenhauer, Royce sought a metaphysics that would permit him to rationally embrace his Christian heritage. Whereas William James was convinced that every demonstrative approach to God must fail, Royce was convinced that speculative reason gives one access to God. The code words of the day, "evolution," "progress," "illusion," "higher criticism," "communism," "socialism," he thought, evoked a mental outlook that reduces Christianity to metaphor and Christian organizations to welfare dispensaries. What was at issue for Royce was not simply a philosophical problem; the philosophers also tutored the architects of the new biblical criticism, the *Redaktionsgeschichte* movement. David Friedrich Strauss, in his *Das Leben Jesu,* under the influence of the Enlightenment, examined the Gospels and the life of Jesus from the standpoint of higher criticism and concluded that Christ was not God, but a supremely good man whose moral imperatives deserved to be followed. This Royce could not accept: there is no philosophically compelling reason, he maintained, to embrace a purely naturalistic interpretation of the sacred scriptures. The movement inspired by Royce was not without success.

By the last quarter of the nineteenth century, nearly every chair of philosophy in the newly emerging universities was held by an idealist. But the intellectual climate was soon to change. Hegel was not able to hold the day in the face of notable achievements in the sciences that demanded recognition of the empirical source of new ways of thinking about nature. Laws of nature are discovered; inquiry is not simply the uncovering of the implicit or the organization of data in the light of the given. To Royce's supposed definitive critique of materialism, opposition was not long in coming. Critiques were mounted in volumes published as corporate philosophical inquiry under titles such as *The New Realism* (1912) and *Critical Realism* (1920), and were soon to control the day. By 1916 the idealism of the St. Louis Hegelians, as they had come to be called, had given way and would soon be replaced by the pragmatic naturalism of John Dewey and his school; Dewey's outlook found expression in another corporate volume, *Naturalism and the Human Spirit* (1944). This signaled the direction the new realism was to take. Under the influence of W. H. Kirkpatrick and Dewey, it became the philosophy undergirding public education in the United States. Not only that, but Dewey's progressive social theory profoundly influenced the shaping of social legislation enacted as part of the New Deal under Franklin Roosevelt and the Great Society initiative under Lyndon Baines Johnson.

In discussing the present influence of Aristotle, it is difficult to separate British and American scholarship, since most English-speaking scholars spend time in North America, often ending their careers in North American universities. The key philosophical issues are largely the same on both sides of the Atlantic. Where Aristotle prevails, metaphysical demonstration of an immaterial order is accepted—so too the immateriality of the human soul and a natural law outlook as the grounding of virtue. The possibility of scientific explanation is taken for granted. Where empiricism prevails, science is reduced to description and prediction; *mind* supplants *intellect* and is accounted for exclusively in terms of brain activity. In the absence of a concept of human nature and the recognition of its *telos,* natural law is supplanted with the values we choose to embrace. So in the end it is not a search for truth, but a transitory state—and one that will itself be replaced by other intellectual currents. At times mainstream academic philosophy seems to be a chaotic scramble to avoid supposed outmoded ontological concepts such as substance, essence, or nature with purely descriptive accounts that remain at a purely empirical level. The idea of an immaterial soul or the concept of a self-existent being, the cause of the existence of things or the concept of an immaterial intellect responsible for the order in nature are rarely entertained apart from antiquarian interest in a given author. Where empiricism prevails, interest in Aristotle is primarily textual exegesis, pursued in the interest of clarity and internal consistency.

This does not mean that Aristotle is not used. Alasdair MacIntyre, in his celebrated book *Whose Justice, Which Rationality?* (1988), shows clearly the ethical implications of an Aristotelian outlook as contrasted with that of David Hume. John M. Rist, in *Real Ethics* (2002), has called for a return to the scientific realism of Plato and Aristotle. Leon Kass, in working out a biomedical ethics (*Life, Liberty and the Defense of Dignity,* 2002), finds it necessary to return to Aristotle's concept of human nature. Contemporary discussions of the Galileo affair often center on whether Bellarmine had the right to demand of Galileo a demonstration in the Aristotelian sense. Nearly all discussions of natural law find it necessary to resort to the metaphysics of Aristotle, but these are largely carried out in those quarters that have never abandoned the study of classical philosophy.

William James, writing at the beginning of the twentieth century, could speak of his Harvard colleagues' "deep appreciation of one another" and of the department's cooperative efforts to convey basic philosophical truths to its students. The Harvard faculty of philosophy at that time included Josiah Royce and George Santayana. Josiah Royce was writing books with such titles as *The Religious Aspect of Philosophy, The World and the Individual,* and *The Problem of Christianity.* Santayana's titles included *The Life of Reason, The Realms of Being,* and *The Sense of Beauty.* James's own *Varieties of Religious Experience* was what we today would call a bestseller. Until the second half of the twentieth century, at least in the United States, philosophy was studied in a more-or-less traditional way. One was expected to know in a cursory way the major figures and movements in the history of Western philosophy. In certain programs, one was also expected to have more than an elementary knowledge of mathematics, physics, chemistry, and biology. Then modernity caught up with the curriculum. Today philosophy has become so specialized that members of the same faculty sometimes find it difficult to communicate with each other. Specialization, it must be acknowledged, reflects a deeper fragmentation of a once integrated discipline in which the parts were clearly understood in relation to the whole. That fragmentation has resulted in many a careful and valuable study of original texts, as can be seen in Aristotelian scholarship alone, but it has also resulted in a kind of trivialization that permits whole careers to be spent on isolated problems in the work of a single philosopher of little consequence, or worse still, on the youthful efforts of a philosopher whose mature works repudiated his early efforts.

When G. E. Moore was asked, "What is the function of philosophy," he could answer, "To give a general description of the whole of the Universe, mentioning all the most important kind of things we know to be in it." C. S. Peirce in his day wanted to be regarded as a laborer in the common enterprise of intellectual inquiry. Peirce is not to be faulted: the division of labor is not the fundamental problem. Given the task of Dame Philosophy, some labor is bound to be subservient. To shift metaphors, the master need not complete every canvas. All profit from the careful analysis and exposition of obscure tests or the production of critical editions of ancient and medieval sources. Yet if one made an empirical survey of the leading North American journals and major university presses, it would be difficult to determine from the articles and books examined the literal meaning of the term "philosophy." Much discourse seems unrelated to the pursuit of wisdom. It is not surprising that the bulk of philosophical work will be unintelligible even to the educated layman, but some work targets an audience no greater than that provided by a handful of university faculties. How many professional philosophers know the difference between a "fallibilistic meliorism" and a "weak version of universal pragmatics"? It may be that we are in our day experiencing the full effects of a turn that took place three centuries ago. Étienne Gilson has remarked that if one starts with the mind, one ends there. "History," says Gilson, is there to remind us that no one ever again regains the whole of reality after locking himself in one of its parts." Tutored by Descartes and others, modern philosophy in repudiating classical philosophy put the epistemological problem first. Josiah Royce, in paying tribute to Leo XIII for his part in the Thomistic revival, expressed the fear that a resurgent Thomism might give way to the Kantian legions and their demand that the epistemological issue be settled first. The issues that confronted the late-nineteenth-century intellectual world remain.

Contemporary studies of Aristotle abound, but few may be considered monumental. Most are published as articles in professional journals and are narrowly focused and unrelated to the Aristotelian corpus as a whole. Conferences and symposia devoted to the study of Aristotle often produce significant volumes. No research library can be without the published results, for example, of an international conference held at Deurne, Netherlands, in 1999, published under the editorship of Frans de Hass and Jaap Mansfield, as Aristotle's *On Generation and Corruption I.* The same is true of significant monographs devoted to specific works of Aristotle, such as Jonathan Barnes's *Aristotle* (1989), Daniel Robinson's *Aristotle's Psychology* (1989), Charlotte Witt's *Substance and Essence in Aristotle* (1989), Fred D. Miller's *Nature,*

Justice and Rights in Aristotle's Politics (1995), and Lloyd Gerson's *Aristotle and Other Platonists* (2005)—and the list could go on. And then there are studies such as Rom Harré's *Varieties of Realism* (1986) and William A. Wallace's *The Modeling of Nature* (1996), which must be regarded as Aristotelian treatises.

These studies attest to the perennial value of the works of Aristotle, who, in spite of relative neglect, remains an indispensable guide in the difficult terrain of metaphysics and epistemology and, one should add, ethics and politics, as well. A little-adverted-to fact is that while technology has broadened the scope of the natural sciences, there have been no similar advances to facilitate the work of philosophy. Instruments from the microscope to the telescope have been augmented in each generation. Particle accelerators with ever-increasing energy have produced startling increases in our knowledge of matter and energy in almost one generation. But in philosophy we are no better equipped than the ancients, who, no less intelligent or observant than we, have much to tell us about nature and human nature from a metaphysical point of view. Aristotle's account of human knowing remains a starting point not easily surpassed. The *Nicomachean Ethics* is of perennial value to the political theorist and continues to serve as a guide to personal fulfillment. The nature and purpose of the polis as described by Aristotle remain a starting point for political theory, even in the age of globalization.

PART ONE

AN ARISTOTELIAN
PERSPECTIVE

HISTORICAL CONTEXT

WHAT IS AT STAKE

The necessity of providing an adequate interpretation of natural science is a task inherited from the eighteenth century, wherein John Locke and David Hume challenged the notions of substance and causality and thereby undermined a classical understanding of science. The awakened Kant accepted Hume's psychological account of causality and went on to ask how science is possible, whereas metaphysics is not. The emphasis Kant placed on the categories as mental structures whose function consisted mainly in organizing data received by the senses had a profound effect on the common understanding of science. Karl Popper's questioning the value of induction may be regarded as a logical consequence.

At the end of the nineteenth century the European philosophical turf was shared by two factions, both coalitions: those of an idealistic strain, largely Hegelians, on one side, and those of a materialistic or skeptical bent, indebted to British empiricism and the Critiques of Kant, on the other. Long eclipsed was the metaphysics of Aristotle and the Schoolmen.

Henri Bergson, in an attempt to confront the skeptical bent

of the mechanistic and deterministic philosophies of his day, philosophies often presented by their adherents as the rational foundation of modern science, developed a metaphysics critical of both Hegel and the empiricists. Bergson was not alone in the search for a way out of the prevailing philosophical climate. In reaction to German idealism, which itself was framed as a reaction to Kant's Critiques, new and critical realisms began to emerge on both sides of the Atlantic. Hegel, initially embraced as an antidote to empiricism, was abandoned when it became clear that Hegelians were hard-pressed to account for the march of new scientific techniques that were leading to remarkable discoveries in the natural sciences. The positivism of Auguste Comte similarly had clear limitations. Comte, schooled in the British empiricism of his day, not only ruled out metaphysics, but ruled out theoretical physics, as well, and both for the same reason: a denial of the efficacy of causal reasoning. According to Comte, physics errs, as does metaphysics, when it postulates abstract entities as explanatory causes. The success of nineteenth- and twentieth-century theoretical physics had yet to undermine positivism as a philosophy of science. Quite apart from its speculative implication, Comte recognized that the social implications of the empiricism emanating from the British Isles led directly to secular humanism, which he codified in his "Religion of Humanity." Parenthetically, it may be noted that Comte is generally accorded the title "Father of Positivism" and is regarded as one of the progenitors of sociology. Although Comte's interests led him away from the philosophy of science per se and into the field of sociology, the term he coined came to be used in the wider sense of a philosophy of knowledge that limited knowledge to sensory experience.

Reflections on the nature and capacity of human knowledge date to the pre-Socratics. Plato's discussion of science and the claims to knowledge by the Greeks will forever remain a starting point of the philosophy of science. It was Plato who bequeathed to Western philosophy the notion that all science is of the universal. Aristotle concurred, but found the universal in nature common to members of the species. Aristotle taught that by a process of abstraction we come to know the essence, quiddity, or nature of a thing, prescinding accidental features that it may or may not have, while the thing remains what it is. Such is the object of science: the nature of an entity, the structure of a process, its properties and potentialities. Yet to have scientific knowledge is not simply to know what is, not simply to have uncovered a law of nature. For Aristotle, to have scientific knowledge is to know the entity, process, or property in the light of its cause or causes. Presupposed by Aristotle are two principles, the principle of causality and the principle of substance, both principles rejected by the British empiricists. The positivism advanced by Comte denies at once the intelligibility of nature and the power of intellect to grasp "the more" that is given in the sense report. From an Aristotelian perspective, there is more in the sense report than the senses themselves are formally able to appreciate. Locke, in denying the reality of substance, reduces what we call substance to a "constellation of events" or sense reports. According to Locke, we use terms that imply substances, but this usage is merely a shorthand way of pointing to something without repeating at length the properties we associate with that something or constellation. David Hume's account of causality similarly limits knowledge to a simple sense report. We experience succession, Hume tells us, not causation. "Cause" is the name we give to the antecedent, contiguous in place, continuous in time, and that we habitually associate with the consequent that we call the "effect."

If there are no natures or substances independent of the mind's creating them, if there is no causality, not only does the enterprise of metaphysics collapse, but modern science is transformed into something other than an attempt to understand nature and its operations in the light of its causes. Metaphysics is based on the assumption that the realm of being is greater or wider in designation than the being reported by the senses. If the material order reported by the senses is all there is, then the most general science of reality is natural philosophy or the philosophy of nature. If there is an immaterial order of being as well as the material world of sense, then the most general science of reality is the philosophy of being known as metaphysics or ontology. One can acknowledge an immaterial order only by a process of reasoning. Such reasoning has led mankind through the ages to affirm the existence of God, to posit an immaterial component of human knowing and a spiritual or immaterial soul.

It is to be noted that the same sort of causal reasoning that leads one to affirm the existence of God also leads one to affirm the existence of the submicroscopic. As Auguste Come himself recognized, causal reasoning is common to both natural theology and theoretical physics. The efficacy of causal reasoning is dramatically seen in those sciences where the postulated entities of one generation become the encountered ones of another. It can be shown that limiting knowledge to the sense report has implications not only for the natural sciences, but for law and the social sciences, as well. On a strict positivist account, science in effect is reduced to description and prediction, thus denying the social sciences their proper object, "human nature."

A historical digression is of use here to illustrate our basic point—i.e., the intellect's ability to grasp the intelligible in the sensory report. Metaphysicians and philosophers of science have devoted many a paper to the seeming irreconcilable discontinuity between the classical and quantum worlds—that is, between Newtonian mechanics and quantum mechanics. From its very introduction it has been recognized that the quantum world of atoms does not operate by the same roles of physics that govern the everyday classical world. Max Planck is credited with introducing the word "quanta" into the lexicon of physics in 1900, and he was to play a significant role in the quantum revolution of the mid-1920s. Acknowledging that a distinction can be made between quantum mechanics and quantum theory, most authors prefer simply to speak of "quantum physics."

There is no obvious point at which the old order of physics gave way to the new order of quantum physics, just as there is no obvious point at which Newtonian physics replaced Aristotle's natural philosophy. Mathematical physics is used to describe how the quantum world operates (quantum mechanics), but explanations of why the quantum world behaves as it does are another thing (quantum theory) and defy the imagination. In classical physics, energy flows in a continuum, but in quantum physics it comes in chunks or quanta, which can only be described mathematically. In the early twentieth century, for most physicists it wasn't necessary to visualize the quantum world, so long as their calculations matched their experimental results. It did not matter that the symbols and mathematics they used might or ought to have any link with the physical world. Nobel laureate Murray Gell-Mann is quoted as saying, "We all know how to use it and apply it to problems; and so we have learned to live with the fact that nobody can understand it."[1] After more than eighty years, physicists are still having trouble reconciling the Newtonian and quantum worlds.

It was the failure of Newtonian physics in the nineteenth century to construct a mechanical or atomic model of matter and ether that would explain thermal and magnetic properties and lead Ludwig Boltzmann to develop his probabilistic physics in a seminal article in 1877 and Planck to introduce the notion of

1. As quoted by L. Wolpert, *The Unnatural Nature of Science* (Cambridge, Mass.: Harvard University Press, 1993), 144.

"quantum" a little more than a decade later. Boltzmann's statistical mechanics not only assumed the existence of invisible molecules, but relied on mathematical probabilities instead of experimental measurements. For that he incurred the scorn of Ernst Mach and the positivists of the Vienna Circle. Mach's positivism, following the lead of Auguste Comte, denied the power of intellect to reason from the seen to the unseen and led Mach to oppose the use of atoms and probabilities in scientific explanation. The only meaningful statements a scientist can make, Mach held, are about what can be measured, counted, or tested or that otherwise rest on the experience of the senses. Mach refused to accept the existence of atoms, even when presented with experimental evidence.

Sheilla Jones, from whom this account is taken, remarks, "*Positivism,* perhaps more accurately called *negativism,* had all but killed theoretical physics in France."[2] Aware of the philosophical landscape at that time, she offers her assessment in a humorous passage: "Positivism has no God and no external world; logical positivism has no God and no external world, but it does have mathematical logic; Kantianism has no external world but does have God; and realism allows for both God and an external world." German mathematicians and physicists of the period, Sheilla Jones tells us, while not philosophically illiterate, did not usually demonstrate philosophical leanings, at least not on the job, and for the most part did not try to bring their scientific activity into logical connection with their philosophy. By 1930, most physicists simply abandoned the need for a philosophical theory of quantum physics. We know that Einstein initially objected to the rules of quantum physics because they appeared to preclude any means of reconciliation with the classical

2. Sheilla Jones, *The Quantum Ten: A Story of Passion, Tragedy, Ambition, and Science* (Oxford: Oxford University Press, 2008), 126.

rules upon which his generalized theory of relativity was based.

Our historical digression apart, it must be acknowledged that a primary task of a philosophy of science is to defend the first principles of thought and being. Those principles can be formulated in different ways. They cannot be demonstrated, but are presupposed by all demonstration. They can be defended. Put simply, they are: Things exist apart from a knowing mind (intelligibility); things are what they are (identity); a thing cannot be and not be at the same time and in the same respect (non-contradiction); a thing is intelligible in terms of itself or in terms of another (efficient causality, sometimes called sufficient reason). These principles are fundamental, and there are none prior to them by which they may be demonstrated. They are principles upon which all demonstration depends, principles that, though they cannot be demonstrated, can be defended. A realist philosophy of science may be regarded as their defense against Locke, Hume, and certain misleading interpretations of relativity theory and quantum mechanics.[3]

The British empiricists, as well as Comte, failed to pay much attention to actual practice in the sciences of their day, practices that in no way and in none of its parts were in accord with their positivist scheme. Reasoning on a causal basis from the observed to the non-observed, then as now, is common practice in the natural sciences. The existence of bacteria was inferred long before the microscope displayed their reality. In physics and chemistry, molecular structures were similarly inferred long before electron microscopes and particle accelerators confirmed their reality.

In the history of theoretical physics, we find successive schema depicting the atom as our knowledge increased. We are led to recognize that our knowledge of nature is open-ended, the focus

3. Cf. Brian Ellis, *The Metaphysics of Scientific Realism* (Montreal: McGill-Queens University Press, 2009).

of an intellectual quest that is never satisfied. In 1933, the state of particle physics was such that it seemed necessary to postulate the existence of a particle as yet undetected. The Italian physicist Enrico Fermi, assuming its existence, built his theory of beta decay upon it and gave the undetected particle a name, "neutrino," Italian for "little one." In spite of the support of Niels Bøhr, he was subjected to remarks about his "poltergeist," since no one had empirically shown it to exist. It remained a hypothetical entity until Clyde Cowan, who with access to a particle accelerator at Hanford, Washington, performed an experiment that confirmed the neutrino's existence. He duplicated the experiment in 1956 at the Savannah River Laboratory in Georgia. The rest is history, for no one today challenges Fermi. I use this example as an illustration of the principle of sufficient reason, sometimes called the principle of efficient causality, where an explanation is sought for something otherwise unintelligible.

It is not misleading to say that in physics causal explanation is taken for granted. The encountered is routinely explained by the non-encountered. No one who examines the course of nineteenth-and twentieth-century physics can affirm that science is simply description and prediction. Scientific knowledge is knowledge in which, under the compulsion of evidence, the mind understands why things are the way they are and not otherwise. Science deals with things considered in their abstract permanence, not with the flux of the singular. It lays hold of what things are, their nature, by means of a process of abstraction in which the intellect grasps the intelligible nature of the object under consideration—a universal nature, not the contingent singular. The contingencies of the singular escape science. Necessities expressed by the universal are the proper object of its grasp. The universality of the object of scientific knowledge is the condition of its necessity. To use Jacques Maritain's poetic way of expressing it, "The sciences of explanation set before the mind intelligibles freed from the concrete existence that cloaks them.... Essences delivered from existence in time."[4] Science is possible because of the mind's ability to abstract from the singular, to capture the universal or intelligible nature common to many, to see the many as a class. The abstractive power of intellect enables us to identify laws of nature and is the basis of all taxonomy. This takes place at the level of what Aristotle and the Scholastics call the first degree of abstraction. Mathematical abstraction is something else.

Modern physics, up to the coming of quantum physics, was commonly spoken of as "Newtonian physics." In the seventeenth century with Newton we entered the age of Galileo, Kepler, Boyle, Halley, Descartes, Gassendi, and Leibniz, intellectual giants all. Seventeenth-century physics, in replacing the qualitative analysis of the ancients with quantitative precision, created a new set of problems. Newton himself wrestled with the problems of how to relate the common and new algebraic analyses of the Moderns with the venerated methods of the ancients. For him, large questions loomed. When is a geometrical construct exact? What guarantees the applicability of geometry to mechanics?[5]

With Descartes and Leibniz, Newton meant to introduce certainty into natural philosophy, the purification of physical science from classical metaphysics, even though it meant parting company with his beloved Plato and Aristotle. Mathematics is the mind's tool or instrument in the whole process. The motions to be studied must be measured and reduced to mathematical formulas. But he resisted what he took to be the anticlassical stance that he perceived in Descartes' *Géométrie* and portrayed

4. Jacques Maritain, *The Degrees of Knowledge,* translated from the fourth French edition by Gerald B. Phelan (New York: Charles Scribner's Sons, 1959), 33.

5. Cf. Niccolò Guicciardini, *Isaac Newton on Mathematical Certainty and Method* (Cambridge, Mass.: MIT Press, 2009).

himself as indebted to Euclid and Appollonius.[6] Furthermore, he tried to reformulate the analytical methods of discovery into a synthetic form, a form in which all references to algebraic analysis are suppressed.

The second degree of abstraction is mathematical abstraction, the kind of abstraction involved when the mind leaves behind not only the singular, but also the determining characteristics of a class to focus only on the entity as a unit or as something possessing extension or a certain configuration. Thus arithmetic and geometry and their derivative sciences come into being. We can speak of "five" and "six," leaving behind the fact that we may counting bells, books, or candlesticks. Similarly we talk about the properties of circles, squares, cones, and straight lines, even though none exists as such in reality. Obviously there are circular, spherical, and conical objects in reality, but none is a perfect exemplar of the idealized abstraction.

Having made the distinction between the two degrees of abstraction, it is necessary to discuss what the Scholastics called intermediate sciences, the physico-mathematical sciences. Physico-mathematical science is not formally physical science, although it is physical as regards the matter in which it verifies its judgments, and although it is oriented toward physical reality and physical causes as the terminus of its investigation. It does not, however, aim to grasp the inner ontological nature of its subject matter. Given the enormous progress made by modern mathematics, it has become more than ever necessary, following Newton's example, to philosophically study the first principles of mathematical science, which alone can provide a rational account of the true nature of mathematical abstraction and the mental objects it considers. Such study would embrace the mutual relationships of the continuous and discontinuous, the real meaning of surds and

6. Guicciardini, *Isaac Newton on Mathematical Certainty and Method*, 386.

transfinite numbers, the infinitesimal, non-Euclidean space, and the validity of mathematical transcripts of physical reality such as quantum mechanics and the theory of relativity.

It is at the third degree of abstraction that the object of metaphysics is attained. At that level the intellect prescinds from every feature, physical and quantitative, to focus on what the whole of reality has in common—namely, being or existence. At this level the mind considers objects of thought that not only can be conceived without matter, but may exist without matter. Metaphysics is a discipline unto itself and beyond the purview of the present treatise.

The distinction between levels of abstraction has implications for our discussion of natural science. There are two possible ways of interpreting the conceptions of modern physics. The one takes their reports literally, just as they are on the philosophical plane, and thereby throws the mind into a zone of metaphysical confusion. The other discerns their spirit, their intentional value, and attempts to determine their proper import. Thus, one may ask, is real space Euclidean or non-Euclidean? Is space postulated by the Einsteinian theory of gravitation real or not? The student of modern physics must be aware of equivocations. The word "real" has not the same meaning for the philosopher as it does for the mathematician and for the physicist. For the mathematician, a space is real when it is capable of mathematical existence—that is to say, when it implies no internal contradiction and duly corresponds to the mathematical notion of space; it duly constitutes a system of objects of thought verifying the axioms of geometry. In a subsequent lecture we will examine at greater length the use and abuse of metaphor in scientific explanation.

For the physicist, space is real when the geometry to which it corresponds permits the construction of a physico-mathematical universe in which all pointer readings are "explained" and at the same time symbolize physical phenomena in a coherent and complete fashion. For a long time, Euclidean space sufficed for the interpretation of physics, but today to interpret the measurements it gathers from nature within which geometry and physics are as far as possible amalgamated, it is necessary to have recourse to spherical and elliptical spaces. For the layman, it is a question of knowing what is real space in the philosophical sense of the word—that is, what is real, as contrasted with an entity of reason.

Euclidean, Riemannian, and other geometrical entities are translatable from one system to another, and all the geometries may be said to be equally "true," but they cannot be real in the philosophical sense of the word. Mathematical intelligibility by itself alone tells us nothing. The straight line of an elliptical plane and a figure that corresponds to a Euclidean model are not different expressions of the same thing. They are intrinsically different entities, belonging to different worlds, and from one of these to the other there is only an analogical correspondence. To affirm the reality of one space is not to affirm at the same time the reality of all the others, but their unreality. Nor will the verification of our senses and our measuring instruments tell us anything about their reality, since with them we quit the mathematical order for the physical order. The mathematical model may serve as a pivotal point, as a model enabling us to correct and interpret the ensemble of measurements taken.

Whereas Euclidean space is directly grasped by intuition, others of necessity are referable to the Euclidean notion of space for their intelligibility. All attempts that have been made to obtain an intuitive representation of non-Euclidean geometries, by Einstein, for example, show that these geometries can be rendered imaginable only by reduction to Euclidean geometry. In sum, non-Euclidean geometries presuppose notions of Euclidean geometry. They offer analogical concepts, with Euclidean concepts providing the primary analogate. In spite of the use that astronomy makes of these geometries, non-Euclidean space is a being of reason. Real geometric space is finite—that is to say, actual existing space is coextensive with the amplitude of the world. Infinite geometric space is a being of reason.

Something similar is encountered in particle physics when physicists form a pure abstract mathematical equivalent of a given atomic structure, a structure that is often unimaginable because it is divested of ontological content. The inferred structure has the characteristic of a fiction, a mere symbol, for the real nature, unknown in itself. The construct is a being-in-reason, although it retains some reference to the being-in-re that led to its postulation.

It comes down to this. A mathematical reading of sensible phenomena cannot speak the last word about the physical real. Physico-mathematical knowledge does not exhaust all that can be known about the physical real. We cannot ask such an account to give an ontological explanation of the sensible real, let alone account for human thought and volition. Tempting though it is, a mechanistic philosophy that endeavors to explain everything in terms of extension and movement neglects an understanding that also cannot be provided by Cartesian philosophy. This is especially true of the spiritual dimension of man, which remains as elusive as ever, though some remain confident that some version of the genome project will eventually shed light on the moral dispositions of a people and on morality itself.[7]

7. The Human Genome Project originated in 1990 and was initially headed by James D. Watson at the U.S. National Institutes of Health. Its purpose was to understand and to map the genetic makeup of the human species. It was thought of as necessary to ensure the continuing progress of medicine and other health sciences. The project was designed to identify the approximate 2,400 genes in the human person, but eventually the authors found it necessary to address some of the ethical, legal, and social issues that arose from the availability of genetic information.

INDUCTION

THE PERENNIAL VALUE OF THE
ARISTOTELIAN PERSPECTIVE

A well-thumbed *Logic* in use through most of the twentieth century is that of H. W. B. Joseph. First published in 1906 at 608 pages, it became the prototype of many a logic textbook written for classroom use. Joseph opens a chapter devoted to the problem of induction with the observation, "The history of the word Induction is still to be written, but it is certain that it has shifted its meaning in the course of time and that much misunderstanding has arisen thereby."[1] Volumes have been written in the last hundred years, but the conflict between the empiricist and the Aristotelian remains the same. Joseph shows clearly what Aristotle in the *Posterior Analytics* understood by induction. "Aristotle," he tells us, "gives the name induction to the formal process of inference by which we conclude a proposition to hold universally of some class, or logical whole, because an enumeration shows it to hold for every part of that whole."[2] This may be called induction

1. H. W. B. Joseph, *Logic* (Oxford: Clarendon Press, 1906), 318.
2. Joseph, *Logic,* 318.

by complete enumeration, or perfect induction. Aristotle shows how it might be thrown into the form of an inductive syllogism. He points out that our knowledge of scientific principles springs historically out of our experience of particular facts, though its certainty rests ultimately on an act of intellectual insight. He gives the name "induction" to the process in which particulars of our experience suggest to us the principles that they exemplify, but this is not a formal process from premises to conclusion. It is not the enumeration that leads us to assent to the universal, but a kind of intellectual penetration.

In Joseph's account, Aristotle goes on to show "where (presumably in default of the necessary insight and assurance from our intellect) we may look for reasons for accepting or rejecting any principles that a science puts forward."[3] He does not give to this procedure, which is of a formal logical kind, the name of "induction," but calls it "dialectic." What he says on this subject is of importance from the standpoint of scientific method and comes close to what modern writers understand by induction. There is no doubt that for Aristotle our knowledge of general principles comes from our experience of particular facts and that we arrive at those principles by induction. Yet the only formal logical process that Aristotle described under the name of induction is that of perfect induction, which clearly neither is nor can be the process by which the sciences establish their laws or general principles. The kinds of reasoning processes or arguments that they really do employ, so far as they appeal merely to the evidence of our experience, are of a different sort.

The strength of Aristotle's treatment of induction became an issue only in modernity, notably after Locke and Hume. Medieval Schoolmen and their contemporary exponents generally consider inductive reasoning unproblematic. The Schoolmen referred

3. Joseph, *Logic*, 391.

to induction as an argument from experience. Albert the Great (1206–1280), for example, writes that our senses teach us the obvious truth about the nature of wine—that it intoxicates—and that our intellect grasps this truth with certainty that cannot be doubted. Modern logicians misunderstand this basic truth when they reduce it to no more than an invalid syllogism. Induction from an Aristotelian perspective, as Joseph shows, is not mere enumeration. Statistical models of induction miss the point when they reduce it to a mechanical process of enumerating cases. Such models fail to appreciate the cognitive leap, the intellectual discernment that produces the intelligible universal. One does not have to examine all instances of copper to understand that copper conducts electricity, conducts heat, and is malleable. The inductive insight is not mere enumeration, a statistical summary, or an endless enumeration. At some point the intellect recognizes that there is more in the sense report than the senses themselves are able to appreciate. Mere multiplication of instances serves no purpose.

One of the best expositions and defenses of the perennial value of the Aristotelian perspective since Joseph is found in three works of Jacques Maritain, which may be read in tandem.[4] Maritain dismisses perfect induction as the purely verbal and sterile form that modern commentators have the naïveté to regard as the only induction known to the ancients.[5] Using his example, we don't have to examine every vertebrate to know what a vertebrate is. We can speak of "vertebrate" as common to man, horse, and crocodile.

4. Jacques Maritain, *An Introduction to Philosophy*, translated from the French by E. I. Watkin (New York: Sheed and Ward, 1937); Maritain, *The Degrees of Knowledge*, translated from the fourth French edition by Gerald B. Phelan (New York: Charles Scribner's Sons, 1959).

5. Maritain, *Formal Logic*, translated by Imelda Choquette (New York: Sheed and Ward, 1937), 270.

It is not from the parts of a collective whole nor from the point of view of a distributed whole or a universal properly so called that we must consider induction if we are to understand it, for induction consists in attributing to an intelligible universal, disengaged, so to speak, by abstraction, a predicate verified by some of the individuals or some of the parts in which the universal is realized. This operation is legitimate when the enumeration of individuals is sufficient and it really furthers knowledge. For to know that every metal conducts electricity is not the same thing as to know that silver, copper are conductors of electricity; it is to know that there is some necessary connection (even though we do not perceive it in itself) between the property and the nature of metal—it is to possess—however obscurely and imperfectly it is nevertheless to possess—a truth *de jure*.[6]

At play here is the distinction between what the Scholastics call the proper object of the senses (sensible properties, color, shape, magnitude, odor) and that of the intellect (a spontaneous insight into the essence or nature of the thing under consideration). We will address this at length in our lecture on the principle of substance.

Maritain has his own way of expressing this insight. He writes, "induction by incomplete enumeration does not make us pass from some to *all* but from some to *every*." We should avoid saying "all metal conducts electricity," and instead say, "metals conduct electricity." It is the intellect's grasp of the nature of metal that enables it to attribute the same predicate to each individual.

Induction has the double function of inference and proof. When considered as an argument or proof, induction admits of a certain zone of probability. It is, in fact, neither an inference properly so-called, nor an argument, nor proof: it merely leads the mind to a connection of terms whose intelligible necessity it perceives immediately: for example, the principle of identity or the principle of causality. Maritain points out that complete induction is a true inference, a true argumentation by which the

6. Maritain, *Formal Logic*, 271.

mind acquires new knowledge. "If modern authors have denied this, it is (1) because as a result of nominalist prejudice they have failed to recognize the nature and value of the universal and thereby the entire process of human knowledge, and (2) because they have understood induction only from the point of view of the parts of a collective whole."[7] It is one thing to know that Peter and Paul are mortals and another to know that man is mortal. By the universal truth that concerns the nature or quiddity common to the enumerated parts, we implicitly possess the raison d'être of the considered property.

Maritain calls attention to a distinction between what belongs to logic itself and what belongs to epistemology or metaphysics. It belongs to metaphysics to discuss nominalism and realism and the controversies concerning the nature of science and ordinary knowledge. The discussion of the first principles of thought and being and the order in which they are known to us is also a part of metaphysics. This we will do in subsequent lectures.

As a personalist, Edith Stein approached the topic from the reverse problem of differentiating or accounting for the individual, given the universal. In her Habilitationsschrift, written under the direction of Edmund Husserl and published posthumously as *Finite and Eternal Being*,[8] acknowledging a common human nature, she tackles the problem of individuation. A person is not simply an exemplification of a common human nature. A person is not like all others with the human form. A person has a level of unrepeatability and dignity that the classic Aristotelian position did not emphasize. This leads Stein into an extended discussion of the principle of individuation. Her position may be described as uniquely her own—neither that of the well-known position of

7. Maritain, *Formal Logic*, 281.
8. Edith Stein, *Finite and Eternal Being*, translated by Kurt F. Reinhardt (Washington, D.C.: The Catholic University of America Press, 2010).

Aquinas nor that of Scotus, who took an entirely different tack. She speaks of "a common human form" where Aquinas would speak of "a common human nature." Although influenced by Aquinas in much of her work, she has a distinctive metaphysical conception of being and essence. She wants to give an account of how there can be many instances of the same type that differ not only numerically, but also qualitatively. She does this by positing a form in addition to the common human form—not exactly Scotus's formal principle of individuation—i.e, the principle of *haecceitas*—but closer to Scotus than Aquinas's *signate matter.* "Stein's primary concern in positing individual forms," Sarah Borden Sharkey explains in her excellent book on Stein, "is not individuation (as such in the case of Scotus's *haecceitas*), the paradigm for being a universal, or identity, but rather uniqueness."[9] To fully understand Stein's position, we would have to review Husserl's theory of parts and wholes as presented in his *Logical Investigations III,* something beyond our present inquiry.

Louis Groarke, in his *An Aristotelian Account of Induction,* develops Maritain's thesis, offering yet another telling critique of the empiricist's account of induction and the empiricist's notion of substance.[10] Like Étienne Gilson and Maritain upon whom he draws, Groarke is conscious of the historical setting of philosophical analysis and debate. He is convinced that no historical idea arrives on the scene without some kind of antecedent. Descartes may have set out to create a new philosophy, both natural and metaphysical, to take the place of Aristotle and St. Thomas Aquinas, yet Jorge Secada, in his careful study of Descartes, finds it necessary to give his book the subtitle *The Scholastic Origins*

9. Sarah Borden Sharkey, *Thine Own Self: Individuality in Edith Stein's Later Writings* (Washington, D.C.: The Catholic University of America Press, 2010), 210.

10. Louis Groarke, *An Aristotelian Account of Induction* (Montreal: McGill-Queens University Press, 2009).

of Modern Philosophy.[11] After Bacon the praise of induction was taken to be a sign of enlightenment. Today popular science writers repeat the all-too-familiar tale about the triumph of modern science over earlier natural philosophy, and the largely uneducated public accepts the story because it lacks the historical knowledge or the philosophical sophistication to wrest itself free of the reigning orthodoxy. In fact, those who did the most to advance the sciences did not refute or even repudiate ancient notions concerning the object of science and the nature of scientific explanation; they merely shifted discourse from consideration of the nature or essence of things to that which can be measured, neglecting to integrate the scientific tableau of the new physics with that of philosophy and common sense.

Pierre Gassendi (1592–1655) is not a household name, but in his own day he was engaged in one way or another with the leading intellectual figures of his period. He corresponded with scores of his illustrious contemporaries, notably with Descartes, Galileo, Kepler, Hobbes, Campenella, and Christina of Sweden. Like others at the threshold of modernity, he was confronted with the problem we have been addressing. He deserves to be remembered, if for no other reason than his cautionary dictum, "It is not permitted to transfer into Physics something abstractly demonstrated in Geometry."[12] Gassendi clearly stands at the threshold of modernity, anticipating the British empiricists by more than a century. It is Descartes and his artificially created "mind/body problem" that stimulated Gassendi to address the age-old problem of universals and the relation between sense and intellectual knowledge. In his criticism of Descartes he writes,

11. Jorge Secada, *Cartesian Metaphysics: The Scholastic Origins of Modern Philosophy* (Cambridge: Cambridge University Press, 2000).

12. Quoted by Antonia Lolordo in Lolordo, *Pierre Gassendi and the Birth of Modern Philosophy* (Cambridge: Cambridge University Press, 2006).

"When you say that you are simply a thing that thinks, you mention an operation that everyone was already aware of—but you say nothing about the substance carrying out this operation, what sort of substance is it, what it consists in, how it organizes itself in order to carry out its different functions."[13] Gassendi's own understanding of nature leads him to a mechanism reminiscent of Epicurus's atomism. Having failed to grasp the fact that much of the moral philosophy he was antecedently committed to could be defended with the metaphysics of Aristotle, he seized upon the philosophy of Epicurus to ground both a theory of knowledge and the inherited moral principles to which he was committed. As a consequence, accounting for the incorporeal, i.e., the existence of God, free will, an incorporeal human soul, and immortality, always remained a problem. Gassendi's difficulty shows clearly that the implications of one's solution to the problem of individuation for ethical theory cannot be overlooked.

Groarke points out that with a textual knowledge of Aristotelian metaphysics, the problem of induction disappears or solves itself. Defending Aristotle against the charge of naïve realism, he is convinced that modern logicians ignore at their peril what medieval philosophers had to say about induction.[14] Hume may have been the first to raise the skeptical doubts about inductive reasoning, but Groarke finds it strange that the problem was overlooked by his predecessors for nearly two millennia. He argues that Locke and Hume and their empiricist followers never attempted a fair understanding of earlier perspectives. There is no textual evidence that Hume had a significant knowledge of Aristotle. In the *Inquiry Concerning Human Understanding* (1739), Hume mentions Aristotle twice, once to emphasize his "utterly decayed" reputation and once in a general reference to the four

13. As quoted by Lolordo in *Pierre Gassendi.*
14. Groarke, *An Aristotelian Account,* 13.

elements.[15] By the time later authors such as Kant and Mill appear on the scene, mainstream philosophy had already lost sight of the original understanding of induction.

If we go back to the Aristotelian texts themselves, Groarke reminds us, we find that Aristotle distinguishes between two different ways of knowing: deduction in which the intellect moves from previously established propositions to a conclusion that follows necessarily, and induction in which the intellect moves from observance of particular instances to general claims about the nature of the thing under discussion. Induction moves from the particular to the universal, whereas deduction involves inference from previously established data. "Scientific induction," writes Groarke, "is for Aristotle a matter of what must be the case; it is the capacity of insight (not argument) that allows us to make logical sense of observation.... Confronted with repeated instances of a phenomenon, human reason arrives at a universal principle, and then goes on to use this universal principle in scientific argument."[16] "Induction is the mental ability to somehow jump from the experience of a particular to concepts, rules, and principles covering a wide variety of cases. We can, then, define Aristotelian induction in two different ways. Induction is, as traditionally understood, an inference from the particular to the universal; but it is also in its most basic form, an inference from sense perception to knowledge. We begin in perception and we end up with words or symbols, with propositions made out of some kind of language, with verbal or linguistic claims that ultimately affirm what is true, in a general way, about the world."[17] Thus we have two different ways of knowing: deduction, in which the intellect moves from previously established propositions to a conclusion

15. David Hume, *Inquiry Concerning Human Understanding,* edited with an introduction by Charles W. Hendel (New York: Macmillan, 1988).

16. Groarke, *An Aristotelian Account,* 27.

17. Groarke, *An Aristotelian Account,* 29.

that follows necessarily; and induction, in which the intellect moves from the observance of particular instances to the nature or essence of the kind of thing in question.

As the Scholastics insisted, it is necessary to keep in mind a distinction between the order of nature and the order of experience. In the order of nature the intelligible nature, the essence, is prior to the sensible fact. To us the particular sensible is known first, and the intelligible principle by which the sensible is explained is known afterward. Induction proceeds from what is first in the order of experience to what is first in the order of nature—from the apprehension of the sensible facts to the apprehension of general principles out of which we subsequently construct the sciences. Without sense experience there is no knowledge of intelligible principles. The process of obtaining knowledge out of sense experience is induction. But there is a difference between apprehension and understanding. Apart from knowing the fact itself, we understand why planets move in ellipses, why some materials burn, why salt dissolves in water only when we have a physical theory that provides a causal explanation. Only by resorting to the principles governing the structure of molecules, by alluding to the atomic structure of salt and water and the laws governing their action, can we understand combustion and solubility. To understand such natural processes as oxidizing and dissolving requires one to understand the underlying causal mechanisms at work. No one will ever see a K-meson or neutrino, but they are among the important non-observables posited in physical theory that enable us to explain a wide range of phenomena. In short, understanding requires an appeal to largely unseen causal mechanisms.

The same is analogously true in the social sciences, where, as in the physical sciences, we need to identify causal mechanisms at work. Peter Manicas, writing from an Aristotelian perspective, addresses the problem of explanation in the social sciences in his *A Realist Philosophy of Science: Explanation and Understanding*.[18] Manicas proves to be a compelling critic of David Hume and the positivism of the Vienna Circle, and by implication their understanding of induction. He defends the thesis that the fundamental goal of both the natural and social sciences is not prediction and control, but rather the understanding of the processes that jointly produce the contingent outcomes of experience. Scientific knowledge, he maintains, consists primarily in knowledge of the internal structures of persisting things and materials and secondarily in knowledge of the statistics of events or the behavior of such things and materials. Scientific understanding occurs when causal analysis enables us to explain how patterns discerned amidst the flux of events are produced by the persisting natures and constitution of things. Manicas makes a distinction between "scientific explanation" and "understanding." Understanding is achieved when explanation includes a well-confirmed theory about the generative mechanism responsible for the phenomena under investigation. Phenomena that are unintelligible in terms of themselves beg to be explained causally. A successful theoretical explanation consists of a representation of the structure of the enduring system in which the events under consideration occur. This is accomplished when the mechanism responsible for its generation is identified.

Drawing heavily on Rom Harré's *Principles of Scientific Thinking* (1970), in which Harré develops an account of explanation in the natural sciences,[19] Manicas analogously employs Harré's thesis as he describes what he calls the "ontological status" of the social sciences. Understanding in the social sciences, Manicas argues, is

18. Peter Manicas, *A Realist Philosophy of Science: Explanation and Understanding* (Cambridge: Cambridge University Press, 2006).
19. Rom Harré, *Principles of Scientific Thinking* (London: Macmillan, 1970).

achieved when, as in the natural sciences, we can exhibit a causal mechanism responsible for the phenomenon in question. He does not deny that there are important differences between the scientific study of nature and the scientific study of society. "In our world, most events—birth, growth, rain, fires earthquakes, depressions, revolutions—are the products of a complex nexus of causes of many kinds, conjunctively at work. It is for this reason that the natural sciences, instead of seeking to explain concrete events, more modestly seek to understand the mechanisms and processes of nature."[20] Without doubt, a social mechanism can be theorized that provides an explanation of why working-class kids get working-class jobs. Typically, suggests Manicas, this would involve identifying their place in society, their beliefs, and their view of the world. Generative social mechanisms in the social sciences are always historically situated. Thus to understand concrete events, such as the collapse of a regime, a depression, or a dramatic increase in divorce, in addition to a pertinent general mechanism, one also needs an historical narrative. "In these cases, explanation takes the form of a narrative that identifies the critical social mechanism and links the sequential to the contingent but causally pertinent acts of persons."[21]

Plato had it right: there is no science of the particular. To explain some event, some actual outcome, one needs to go back in time and identify sequentially the pertinent causes that produce that outcome. To understand Western culture, one needs to examine the classical and Christian origins of that culture and its development through time. To understand Islam one needs to examine the life and teachings of the Prophet, the Hadiths, and the history of Islamic conquest. "This will require," as Manicas insists, "a narrative that links critical actions and events with on-

20. Manicas, *A Realist Philosophy,* 3.
21. Manicas, *A Realist Philosophy,* 5.

going social processes grasped in terms of social mechanisms."[22] In history there are no laws or sets of conditions from which one can make deterministic calculations. An explanation of any event requires the identification of the causal mechanisms at work in the social order. Understanding comes when we have a well-informed theory about the relevant generative mechanism.

I trust that this lecture with the above historical excursions has not only clarified Aristotle's treatment of induction, but has shown that any resolution to the problem of induction, be it from the perspective of Wittgenstein's positivism, Edith Stein's personalism, or Gassendi's atomism, is one that has implications for the way we view many other things—notably, scientific explanation. But the implications are not limited to the natural sciences, for those accounts influence our understanding of human nature and the social order in its moral and cultural dimensions.

22. Manicas, *A Realist Philosophy*, 183.

PART TWO

BASIC PRINCIPLES

THE PRINCIPLE OF SUBSTANCE

⌒

The thesis to be advanced in this lecture is that Aristotle's doctrine of substance is as relevant today as it was when it was first propounded. It must be acknowledged at the outset that ideas have a life of their own, and this is no less true of certain key Aristotelian notions. Aristotle becomes more sophisticated in the commentaries of the Scholastics and still more sophisticated in the twentieth century. Indeed, some of the best contemporary work in philosophy is nothing other than the creative appropriation of the classical past and its medieval commentators. The ancients no less than we were acute in observation, precise in making distinctions, and careful in drawing implications. Where the problems haven't changed, good answers elicit perennial appreciation; good solutions require acknowledgment.

Of course, this view is not shared by all. Reinhardt Grossman, in his "attempt to give a complete and accurate list of the categories of the world," writes, "The nineteenth century sees the final destruction of the Aristotelian ontology. Not just one, but several new categories appear on the ontological stage: relations, structures, classes, and facts."[1] It is easy to show that Grossman is wrong: that Aristotle's basic insights remain intact, and that his so-called new categories are ancient ones, indeed.

Aristotle employs the notion of "substance" to account for a multiplicity of phenomena. Unless otherwise indicated, "substance" will be employed here in the Aristotelian sense of "second substance," as contrasted to "supposit" or "existent." Depending upon the insight to be conveyed, second substance may also be called "essence" or "nature." The distinction between substances and accidents enables Aristotle to distinguish between changes that merely modify and changes that remove a thing from its class. Furthermore, in the order of explanation, it provides an account of the reception and the conferral of action and an account of how a multiplicity of qualities can exist in the same subject. Importantly, it suggests an analogue for inquiry into "social" as opposed to "natural" processes and structures.

These several theses are but aspects of a unified theory of being and knowing. They are defended neither in isolation from their ontological roots nor in ignorance of their implications, yet not all that is presupposed here can be defended within the brief span of this presentation. While the vantage point that governs this inquiry is only one of many strands discernable in the Western intellectual tapestry, it is taken as one required by both ordinary and scientific inquiry. To formulate questions in a certain way is to invite certain answers. If we ask the twin questions (1) "How can the individual in the order of activity change and yet remain the same individual?" and (2) "What does it mean to achieve scientific knowledge?" both questions inevitably lead to the invocation of ontological structures recognized in the Aristotelian corpus. To tackle the latter question first is a decidedly

1. Reinhardt Grossman, *The Categorial Structure of the World* (Bloomington: Indiana University Press, 1983), xvi.

un-Aristotelian move, but for the purposes at hand, my infidelity may be justified.

Let us speak first about the nature of knowledge, particularly scientific knowledge. If one assumes that the aim of science, as we have previously suggested, is to find the structures or states from which the phenomena of nature flow, then scientific knowledge consists of two main types of information. As Rom Harré has argued, scientific knowledge consists (1) in knowledge of the internal structures of persisting things and materials and (2) in the knowledge of the statistics of events, of the behavior of such things and materials, wherein one discerns patterns among these events through certain types of change, but not through other kinds.[2] Emphasis is placed on structures and their persistence. The recognition of such units and their differentiation is the recognition of natural kinds. The chemical analysis of a material, the genes inherited from a parent, the structure of a crystal, the electronic configuration of an atom, point to real structures and to real essences. In them reside the powers of generation and production through the operation of which the flux of events results. That is, a scientific exploration consists essentially in accounting for the second type of information in terms of the first. In a scientific exploration, we show how the patterns discerned among events are produced by the persisting natures and constitutions of things. On this account, the actual world is neither a Parmenidean sphere of unchanging unity nor a Heraclitian flux of free-floating events. The world consists of numerous, fairly permanent units, having internal features and being parts of larger structures that persist. As Aristotle saw, the persistence in existence of these structures doesn't need to be explained, but the changes that take place among them do require explanation.

2. Rom Harré, *The Principles of Scientific Thinking* (Chicago: University of Chicago Press, 1970), 5ff.

There are many ways in which we mentally capture and communicate our knowledge of the structures under consideration. We use sentences to represent and communicate linguistically. But linguistic vehicles are not the only vehicles of thought. Pictures, models, and diagrams are also vehicles of thought.[3] To draw a diagram or to make a model is to think. To construct a diagram, a picture, or a model is an attempt to visualize the inner structure or constitution of a thing. The twentieth-century preoccupation with linguistic vehicles such as declarative sentences and hypothetical propositions has blinded us to the structural picture from which they have been abstracted.[4] Conditional statements are more apt to call attention to the possibilities of change, to the successive states of things, than to the structure of the things themselves. The two approaches, needless to say, are complementary: structure may be presented diagrammatically by means of pictures and models; the possibilities of change may be presented as conditional statements. A structure can be brought to mind by being described, but conditionality cannot be pictured. Verificationist theories of meaning assume that the only form of our knowledge is sentential. For the verificationist, to know the meaning of a scientific proposition is to know what might be considered evidence for that proposition. Historically, verificationism has been closely connected with a positivism that views all science as nothing more than the description of the regularities in human experience. Aristotle saw that the subject

3. Harré, *Principles of Scientific Thinking*, 12.

4. Harré defends this view at considerable length. Speaking of the Aristotelian position, he writes, "In keeping with this view of theories would be the view that scientists are at least as much concerned with the discovery of structures and constitutions as they are with the discovery of regularities in the course of events and with trying to discover how things behave. On this view the vehicle for scientific thought are not only propositions, but pictures, models and diagrams as well, because these latter control, to a large extent, what propositions appear in the heart of a theory"; Harré, *Principles of Scientific Thinking*, 15.

matter of science is not simply a sequence of events. Some science does more than just describe. Thus the vehicles of scientific thought cannot be exclusively propositions. If the inner structure and constitution of things are reached in scientific knowledge, this needs to be acknowledged in accounts of such knowledge.

Pictures, models, and diagrams are metaphors or forms of analogy not unlike those we employ in ordinary discourse. In scientific as well as in ordinary speech, analogy functions to make available the less known in terms of the better known. Natural science is so permeated with metaphor that its employment goes almost unnoticed. Lord Kelvin once said that he could not understand anything except insofar as he could construct a model. In physics, we speak of light *waves,* talk about heat as *fluid,* gases as if they consisted of plastic *particles,* electricity as a *current, drops* of electricity, *anti-matter, right-handed* and *left-handed spin* on a K-meson; we talk of Faraday's *strained space,* electron quantum *jumps,* and star *creation.* In spite of the widespread employment of metaphor in the sciences, one encounters few theories of their function.

Theories of analogy first came into being in an attempt to understand how metaphysics could speak of things divine and not slip either into agnosticism or anthropomorphism. Analogy is a mean between the extremes of univocity and equivocity. When the meaning of a term is identical in the several instances in which it is employed, there is not expansion of meaning, but only routine identification. On the other hand, where meaning is completely equivocal, nothing has been revealed. This is not to suggest that common metaphors in the sciences function in exactly the same way as they do in ordinary discourse.

In ordinary prescientific knowledge, just as in scientific knowledge, metaphor plays a heuristic role, revealing semi-disclosed aspects of things and suggesting new ways to look at things. Perhaps it should be put the other way around: the scientific employment of metaphors, analogies, and models is not unlike their use in everyday coming-to-know. The value of a prescientific knowledge of things and processes tends to be underacknowledged. Overlooked is the continuity between the two types. Things and processes that form the object of scientific knowledge are known in a vague or imprecise manner before they become objects of the controlled and systematic knowledge that is science. As we have seen, one of the unfortunate effects of certain nineteenth-century theories of science was to place the emphasis upon mathematics and experiment divorced from our personal contributions in using them, thus creating a gulf between science and life.

Considerations of our knowledge of nature, it is suggested, lead to the recognition of natural structures. But are those structures ultimate? The question regarding ultimacy is obviously a question of a different order. To answer it, it is necessary to go back to Aristotle's analysis of change and to the metaphysical structure it reveals. A theory of being is drafted as he attempts to explain change. The multiplicity of distinctions he introduces in his attempt to account for becoming give him not only a theory of reality, but a theory of knowledge, as well.

Locke and Hume deny the reality of structures apart from the mind. Even an empiricist of the stature of George Santayana, commenting on Hume's view of substance, writes: "When modern philosophers deny material substance, they make substances out of the sensations or ideas which they regard as ultimate facts.... They deny substances in favor of phenomena which are hypostatized because phenomena are individually wholly open to intuition."[5] Santayana had his own reasons for dismissing Hume; in part they are not unlike the reasons that will be given here.

5. George Santayana, *Scepticism and Animal Faith* (New York: Dover, 1980), 19.

Santayana himself thought that substance as a category is needed to understand the flux of events.

John H. Randall, Jr., in his presidential address in 1964 to the Metaphysical Society of America, gave a modified Humean analysis of substance. There he reaffirmed a position he had taken seven years earlier in the pages of *The Review of Metaphysics*.[6] In that article, "Substance as Process," Randall attempts to reconcile Dewey and Aristotle. Dewey had taken the view that qualities and complexes of qualities are simply the qualities they are and not attributes of something other than themselves. "Substance," Randall suggests, is the name we give to a constellation of events. Inquiry creates the substances it deals with. Substance is that part of the process in which we have an interest at the moment. Substance is thus "subject matter."

Randall's approach, however, fails to raise a fundamental question. That question is, how can an individual change in the order of activity and yet remain the same individual? Not all change removes a being from its class. Some changes are simple modifications in a being that remains "essentially" the same throughout the change. To such changes we give the name "accidental" as distinct from "substantial." A substantial change occurs when a thing is removed from its class. Aristotle accounts for such changes by means of the principles of matter and form. On the other hand, change that merely modifies requires the recognition of a different kind of composition, namely, that between subject and modification—that is, between substance and accident. The composition is not between beings that are, but between principles of being. Metaphysically described, substance is the subject, or remote potency, out of which is educed an accidental form. Every accidental change effects an actuation of the

6. John H. Randall, Jr., "Substance as Process," *Review of Metaphysics* 10 (June 1957): 580–601.

substance. Each modification is a limited expression of the further actuality of its subject. The new actualities "happen" to an individual being, happen to a subject. "Standing under" is thus an inappropriate metaphor to convey the reality, and, it might be added, is a metaphor that has led to much mischief in the history of philosophy, because it tends to hypostatize substance. Substance here understood is both a principle of potentiality and a principle of limitation. We may say that the subject is potential to its happenings. There is something in the subject that permits these happenings, but at the same time functions as a principle of limitation with respect to what can happen. The extent or degree of the happening will depend on the particular kind of substance in which it occurs. Because substance places a limitation on accidental perfection, a substance can enjoy a multitude of accidental perfections. If substance did not place a limit on accident, if there were not a real distinction between the two, every being would be totally in act with respect to every perfection it could possibly have. Or put another way, if the substance did not place a limitation on the act secondarily added, that act would be possessed completely, and hence the subject would be in a state of pure act. I am not saying that Aristotle himself developed his doctrine in this language. There is more in Aristotle's doctrine of substance than he himself articulated. We owe to Aquinas a distinction between quiddity and the act of *to be*, between essence and existence, a distinction that enables us to see substance in a new light.[7]

On Thomas's view, if action were really identified with the subject of action, there could be no potency in the subject, and we would have to say that the subject has its own *to be*. But the

7. Thomas Aquinas, *De Ente et Essentia,* chap. I-II. For an extended discussion of the Thomistic notion of substance, see Charles A. Hart, *Thomistic Metaphysics* (Englewood Cliffs, N.J.: Prentice Hall, 1959), chaps. 7-9.

things of our experience are not their own acts of *to be.* They come into being and they pass away. Consequently the action that we call accident must be recognized as really distinct from its subject. Action on this view must be said to be act with regard to the potency of the substance. The actuation of a substance occurs according to the capacity of the substance, or according to the substance's potency toward act.[8]

Being, predicated on substance and accidents, is not predicated in a univocal, but in an analogous manner.[9] Aristotle saw this. He did not make the mistake of looking upon being as if it were a genus with ten species. If being were a genus, it would have to be predicated of its subclasses or species in exactly the same sense. Accidents from an Aristotelian point of view do not have being in the same sense as substance. An accident is only a being of a being, an *ens entis.*

It goes without saying that substance in the sense here employed is not an object of sense experience. What the senses perceive is substance modified by its accidental features. The reality of substance is recognized as a result of reflection on experience. Substance is a principle of being, not a being or being itself. What the impression reveals is not *this man* or *this whiteness,* but a white something, a something colored, a something extended—that is, the substance, the colored, the extended. The intellect tells us that something is colored or extended. The senses know nothing about being and its principles. The intellect,

8. Thomas Aquinas, *Summa Contra Gentiles,* II, c. 52, translated by Anton C. Pegis as *On the Truth of the Catholic Faith,* 5 vols. (Garden City, N.Y.: Hanover House, 1955–1956).

9. Cf. Joseph Owens, "The Expressions of Entity," in *The Doctrine of Being in the Aristotelian Metaphysics,* 189–98 (Toronto: Pontifical Institute of Mediaeval Studies, 1957); see also Owens, "Aristotle on Categories," in *Aristotle: The Collected Papers of Joseph Owens,* edited by John R. Caton, 14–22 (Albany: State University of New York Press, 1981).

however, sees the necessity for distinguishing between the determinations of the subject and the subject of these determinations. Presupposed is the distinction between sense and intellectual knowledge. Obviously an argument on behalf of the reality of substance would have little value against anyone who denied the distinction between sense and intellect.

Substance as here conceived is obviously not an inert substrate. It is of the very character of limited being to demand further actuality. From a Thomistic point of view, essence as possible existence is not only potential with respect to the act of *to be,* but with respect to further perfection—acts secondarily added. Yet substance is not immediately potential to accidents. The potential and actual state of a thing in any instance must be in the same predicament. Potential substance when actualized is substance. Similarly, the actualization of an accident is not more than an accident. Acknowledging this, we must posit certain potentialities for accidents that are the immediate source of all actions for finite beings. Potentialities or powers to act are themselves accidents. In rational beings, they are called faculties. Powers are intermediary between the subject and its actions. The ultimate source of both powers and actions is, of course, the existing substance or supposit. For without the supposit, none of them could exist. All actions are of the supposit.

Powers are required of all beings whose *to be* is not identical with their act. They are not of the essence of substance, but they flow necessarily from it. Because they flow necessarily from the essence of substance, they are called proper accidents or simply properties. They come into existence with the supposit and endure as long as the supposit itself. The activities of the being inhere, not immediately in the supposit, but in powers to act, and through them in the supposit. Actions immediately actualize an accident—namely, a power to act. The supposit is really actualized by its powers. These powers have their being in the substance that they further actuate.

As previously noted, a distinction is relevant between substance considered as a principle of operation (nature) and substance considered in its completeness (supposit). "Supposit" is the individual, Aristotle's first substance. It suggests the notes of concreteness, completeness, autonomy, and incommunicability. It is the first subject of all predication. For Aquinas there is nothing about the nature of substance considered abstractly that requires that it be a support of accidents. Only limited or finite substances demand additional perfection. The Thomistic notion of substance, for example, does not imply limitation. When essence limits the act of *to be,* substance will necessarily require additional perfection. Where essence is not a limiting principle, but is identical with the act of *to be,* further perfection would be impossible.

At the beginning of this lecture I suggested that models, pictures, and diagrams are created in an attempt to understand the natures of things. In some instances they may be little more than mnemonic aids, but more often than not they express insights into structures that exist independently of the mind. Since knowledge is an ongoing process, no model is ever likely to be complete. The ontological richness of even the simplest structure is apt to require revision after revision. We can never plumb the depths of the beings that we encounter. If biography after biography is sometimes required to fathom the personality of a great person, so too the science of century after century may be required to intellectually approximate nature's structures. Model supplants model, each taking cognizance of new discoveries. It is rare that the false is supplanted with the true; rather, the less adequate account is usually replaced by the more adequate.

Permit me now to make a distinction, lest it be supposed that

I have been identifying structure with the Aristotelian concept of essence. Structure is not a synonym for essence. Structure is in the order of accident; it is an arrangement of parts outside of parts in space. When adequate, models approximate structure. We had a visual model of the cell long before we saw it with a microscope. The double-helix molecule, responsible for the inheritance of genetic traits, was an iconic model long before the electronic microscope confirmed its existence. The inference to many chemical and subatomic structures has been supported in a plurality of ways as our instruments have become more sophisticated. As our knowledge of the structures of things becomes more perfect, we can understand why things behave as they do. But no matter how revealing structure may be, it is not metaphysically ultimate.

For processes, structure may be ultimate, but processes themselves consist of components that need to be analyzed. The component of a structured process is itself a structure. Often more than one model is needed to depict all we know about a given entity; the quiddity depicted is richer than any one model can intimate. Structure is one attempt to articulate what is grasped. This is not to say that structure does not explain a great deal. If we know the structure of a molecule or an organism we can make a great many predictions about it. But ontologically, structure presupposes the parts that are structured. Aristotle's doctrine of form and matter accounts for the nature of that which is structurally determined in a given way. In one sense structure may be called a proper accident, since structure follows nature. But structure *can* be modified without changing the thing fundamentally. Electron orbits can be modified without destroying the atom. Legs and limbs can be amputated, organs removed without destroying the organism. Perhaps there is a note of equivocation here. Implicitly there seems to be a distinction between essential structure and accidental structure. Pruning a tree in some sense alters the structure of the tree, but doesn't affect the specific nature of the tree. The nature of the thing and its concomitant structure permit so much and no more change in the arrangement of, or loss of, parts. The arrangement must still conform to a specific structure, or the thing will pass out of existence. Aristotle held that alteration disposes a substance to be corrupted. If hydrogen atoms are excited, there is a tendency for them not only to change qualitatively, for example, in color, but to become something else. If the electron of a hydrogen atom is excited far enough from its nuclear center, the hydrogen will be destroyed and become a proton with the electron freed from its nuclear influence, and both proton and electron will tend to be absorbed into some other atom. Have we reached the point where we are willing to say that the structures postulated or described by the sciences are really nothing other than Aristotle's form? Form is the principle of actuality in the essence, but it is not act without limit. Matter limits form and in doing so determines the resulting structure. In Aristotelian terms, structure cannot be understood simply as form. Structure results from the union of form and matter, and as such is in the order of accident, although it may be said to flow necessarily from the principle of actuality in the essence.

This manner of speaking may be foreign to contemporary ears, but, I maintain, not because there are any intrinsic difficulties with it, but because certain questions are not raised. Those among the ancients who were dissatisfied with the then-current atomisms or mechanisms were dissatisfied because those philosophies did not answer all the questions asked. If those questions are indeed asked, atomism and mechanism fail. In contemporary philosophy of science there is a movement afoot that amounts to a return to realism. It is a major challenge to the positivism of a previous generation. Two recent late-twentieth-century books may be taken as examples. D. M. Armstrong in his book *What Is a Law of Nature?* spends a great deal of time defending a realistic interpretation of science.[10] So, too, does Ian Hacking in his study *Representing and Intervening.*[11] Without actually saying so, Rom Harré has returned to a strict Aristotelianism.[12]

The major aim of this lecture has been to suggest that an Aristotelian realism, given its empirical grounding, is no less relevant today than it was in antiquity. It remains true today to say that the proper object of scientific knowledge is the essence (call it nature or substance) of natural things. That the object of science is the permanent common nature is supported by an analysis of change that recognizes persistence amid change and accounts for it by means of two sets of principles. There is nothing in contemporary science that forces us to abandon Aristotle's analysis. If we raise Aristotelian questions, we still get Aristotelian answers.

10. D. M. Armstrong, *What Is a Law of Nature?* (Cambridge: Cambridge University Press, 1983).

11. Ian Hacking, *Representing and Intervening* (Cambridge: Cambridge University Press, 1983).

12. Harré, *Principles of Scientific Thinking.*

POTENTIALITY
UNCOVERED

The ability to deal with the concept of potentiality is a major test for any philosophy of science. Few will deny that capacities, dispositions, propensities, or tendencies are real. It is how these are to be understood that divides philosophers into camps. Whitehead's use of the term "potentiality" and its correlative "actuality" is different from that of Aristotle. Locke's "constellation of events" metaphysics differs from Nicholas Rescher's conceptual idealism. How one answers the question, "In what sense are potentialities real?" is indicative of one's metaphysical outlook. An answer not only divides idealist from realist, but metaphysician from logician. There is ample evidence that those who write about "possible worlds" tend to blur, if not confuse, logical and material possibility. Logicians, by trade, are inclined to pay little or no attention to the way premises are obtained. Logic deals with judgments as it finds them; its subject matter is the given. Since mathematical truths are universal and necessary, the temptation is to think of them as eternal and relate them to the actual as if the relation were that of the determinable to the determinate. The temptation is to speak of existence as a determination that happens to a possible essence. Thus whatever is logically possible becomes a candidate for instantiation.

The careful logician will, of course, avoid the trap. He is aware that the manifold of merely possible things is an intellectual construct, and that the starting point of this construct is an informed view of the real world as provided by the sciences. The realist recognizes that intellectual construction is subject to the implicit constraint of the given. One must acknowledge the distinction between real or physical possibility and the strictly hypothetical. The physically possible is governed by the laws of nature. Even from a logical point of view, the really possible is that which is consistent with a certain body of stipulated fact, but how to determine that consistency? Is all that is not intrinsically self-contradictory possible? As long as we remain in the order of abstract possibility, whatever is not contradictory is said to be possible. But as soon as we enter the order of existence, impossibilities begin to multiply. If existence is imparted to any one structure, some others become impossible.

This difference may be illustrated by that between the artist and the art critic. Artists, be they poets, painters, sculptors, or musicians, function within an existential situation. The "form" is either "found in the marble," to use Michelangelo's image, or dictated by material contingencies. The critic, not so constrained, is free to imagine possibilities contrary to the structure or conditions available to the artist. Who has not experienced the critic who, in the light of ideals inappropriate or impossible to meet, finds fault with the art work before him? Something like this occurs in the political order when the ideal is allowed to drive out the good. In human experience there are no fully determined essences prior to their actual instantiation. They cannot be what they are unless they first become it. The key word from an Aristotelian perspective is "finding," not "supposition."

From a realist perspective, if we talk about possibilities we do not ordinarily concern ourselves with logical possibility. Logical and mathematical truths are universal and necessary possibilities, and about them we do not deliberate. Nor do we normally deliberate about a creative imagination at play. Creative imagination feeds on intelligible factors drawn from experience, but is not bound to their natural order.

From an Aristotelian perspective, it is capacity, tendency, and disposition on the part of physical objects that are at once the ground of logical possibility, artistic imagination, and the object of scientific inquiry. In determining what is materially possible, appeals are made to empirically ascertained law—that is, to laws of nature or to statistical evidence derived from what has been the case. The potentialities recognized in things are more or less permanent features of those things. They are predicated of those things whether or not they are acting or being stimulated from without. We utilize copper tubing because of its resistance to corrosion or because of its ability to conduct heat efficiently and, similarly, copper wire because it is capable of conducting electricity. "Fragile," asserted of crystal, indicates something of the structure of the crystal, and the feature indicated is determined by means other than dropping the glass. The capacity to break does not consist in the occurrence of the event. It seems forced to construe fragility in modal terms, such that we say or imply something like: "A fragile piece of glass is one that would break in some possible world in which, unlike the present world, it is actually being dropped." The reason that we believe that a certain disposition can be asserted of a subject is that we know that it currently has such and such a capacity or power. Thus to ascribe a power to a thing or material is to say something about what it can do. To merely specify external conditions is not enough. Circumstances may change without affecting the thing itself. To ascribe a power is to ascribe a disposition to a specific subject because we have some insight into the nature or structure of the thing.

The term "magnetic" is an example of a dispositional term. It designates not a directly observable characteristic, but rather a disposition on the part of some physical object to display a specific reaction under certain circumstances. Take the conditional definition of magnetic—i.e., "If a small iron object is close to x at time t, then x is magnetic at t, if and only if, that object moves toward x at t." I submit that when we predicate "magnetic," we mean more than to just specify a condition. The vocabulary of natural science abounds in dispositional terms such as "malleable," "elastic," "fissionable," "recessive trait," and the like. Are these features not as real as any empirically observed property that we may predicate? Does not structure as disclosed through previous behavior manifest inherent disposition? From an Aristotelian perspective, a nature is manifested through its activity. The whatness or essence of a thing is disclosed by its behavior. The causal inference to the nature responsible is unavoidable. Also unavoidable is the inclination to form some sort of conceptual aid as we attempt to understand the mechanism responsible for the activity under consideration. Those who favor a contextual approach merely describe, not explain.

The subjunctive conditional, while not inaccurate, nevertheless flies in the face of the way we normally think and speak about things. The ghost of David Hume haunts Carnap and his contemporary disciples who elect the modal interpretation. Their understanding of "potentiality" is consistent with their repudiation of classical metaphysics. An Aristotelian will affirm not only that being, but being in act, is intelligible. We do not need to settle for a chronicle of things past and a chart of expectations; we need a theory that explains behavior. Only by recognizing a physical connection between the nature of a thing and the way it acts do we find the root of the conceptual connections employed in talk of material and logical possibility.

Probing deeper, from an Aristotelian perspective the structure of an entity (it may be the shape of a living entity or an inferred electron configuration) is the immediate effect of its nature. Structure is to be distinguished from that which is structured; for example, because of its structure, magnesium has a low density, is disposed to react with most acids to liberate hydrogen, and is resistant to most alkalis. Furthermore, it is disposed to form compounds of a certain kind where it can exhibit a plus-2 oxidation state. Other features can be identified, and these are frequently expressed by means of dispositional terms. If this is granted, we need not suppose that every capacity or disposition identified requires the attribution of a power. There is reason to argue that diverse dispositions may be manifestations of the same power. In fact, dispositions attributed to a thing may be nothing more than structure viewed from several vantage points. On the other hand, as we move from atom to molecule, to compound, to organism, powers are more easily discerned, particularly when the subject is animate.

Since antiquity, cognitive and appetitive powers have been distinguished, and both distinguished from the purely vegetative. The list has never been long, and always where encountered, identification follows empirically derived evidence. The Scholastic axiom succinctly expresses the thought that powers are specified by behavior, behavior by its object. Nothing is inferred, nothing predicated of a subject unless demanded by the evidence. The process of attribution and, negatively, of elimination is by no means simple. The lower the order of being, the more constant or invariable the nature will appear. The more sophisticated our knowledge of a thing, the more we understand the mechanism to confer and receive. In dealing with relatively simple structures at the atomic or molecular level, the identification of the molecular structure may be simply the identification of the power. Molecular structure may itself be the only feature we need to recognize in order to account for the physical or chemical behavior discerned. Structure itself is, after all, a disposition of parts. The more we know about those parts and their relation to each other, the more we can determine what is possible. To say this is not to subscribe to a mechanistic or atomistic interpretation of nature, such as that we found in Pierre Gassendi, but to recognize that powers are closely related to the natures that manifest them. Some philosophers of science would banish altogether the notion of power and settle for a purely descriptive account. But to the realist, the distinction between thing and disposition, between disposition and activity, are real, and when acknowledged, assist in rendering intelligible the phenomena to be explained.

As Rom Harré has argued, scientific knowledge consists primarily in a knowledge of the internal structures of persisting things and materials, and in the knowledge of the statistics of events, of the behavior of such things and materials, wherein one discerns patterns among these events through certain types of change and not through other kinds. Emphasis is placed on structures and their persistence. The recognition of such units and their differentiation is the recognition of natural kinds. The chemical analysis of a material, the genes inherited from a parent, the structure of a crystal, the electronic configuration of an atom, point to real structures, to real natures or essences. In them reside the powers of generation and production. Through their operation the flux of events unfolds. On this account, a scientific explanation consists primarily in accounting for the second type of information in terms of the first. A scientific explanation shows how the patterns discerned amid the flux of events are produced by the persisting natures and constitutions of things.

On this account, the actual world is neither a Parmenidean sphere of unchanging unity nor a Heraclitian flux of free-floating events. The world consists of numerous, fairly permanent units, having internal features and being parts of larger structures that persist. As Aristotle saw, the persistence in existence of these structures doesn't need to be explained, but the changes that take place among them do require explanation.

A subsequent lecture will be devoted to causal explanation, but this much needs to be said at this point. If we distinguish between understanding and explanation, understanding comes when explanation includes a well-confirmed theory about the generative mechanism responsible for the phenomena in question. A successful theoretical explanation consists of a representation of the structure of the enduring system in which the events under consideration occur. Phenomena unintelligible in terms of themselves beg to be causally explained, and this is accomplished when the mechanism responsible for their generation is identified. In the natural sciences, it is the role of theory to provide representation of the generative mechanisms responsible for the observed. Quantum theory, for example, offers generative mechanisms for observed processes. Molecular chemistry is employed to explain organic growth. Theories that represent generative mechanisms give us understanding. The natural sciences have as their object not concrete events, but the processes of nature. As Plato pointed out, there is no science of the singular; all science is of the universal. We understand, for example, why planets move in ellipses, why materials burn, why table salt dissolves in water when we have a physical theory that provides an explanatory mechanism. This is accomplished when we are able to provide principles detailing the structure of molecules, the atomic structure of salt and water, principles of their action, and so on. So equipped, we understand the causal mechanism at work responsible for the oxidation, the dissolving, combustion, and solubility. Causal mechanisms are often inferred, never visually encountered, but they are among the important non-observables posited in physical theory that facilitate understanding. Enrico Fermi, years before the actual discovery of the neutrino, incorporated the inferred particle in his theory of beta decay.

Understanding in the social sciences is similarly achieved when, as in the physical sciences, we can exhibit a causal mechanism responsible for the phenomena in question. There are important differences between the scientific study of nature and the scientific study of society. As we have seen in the previous lecture, the task of the social sciences is to understand the social mechanisms at work with the production of a determinate outcome. Generative social mechanisms of social processes are always historically situated and partake more of the particular than of the universal. Social science seeks to explain concrete events and episodes. The generative mechanisms of social processes are the actions of individuals. Explanation takes the form of a narrative that identifies the critical social mechanisms that link them sequentially to the contingent, but causally pertinent acts of persons. Understanding presupposes good descriptions, both of a quantitative and qualitative character. History is a special case. In history there are neither laws nor sets of conditions from which one makes determinate calculations. To explain some de facto event, one needs to go back in time and identify sequentially the pertinent causes as they combined to produce the outcome. This requires a narrative that links critical actions and events with ongoing social processes grasped in terms of social mechanisms.

That we do in fact successfully convey information about things to other speakers of the language is incontrovertible. But how do we achieve such accuracy, correctness, and objectivity in spite of metaphor? What is the ontological basis for successful communication? If we examine this problem for a moment, we find that in making a simple descriptive statement, we draw the listener's attention to some more-or-less specific feature of an object and convey some information about it. Basically two kinds of information may be conveyed. One kind says that whatever is referred to is like certain other things in some respects—that is, it belongs to a certain class; the other kind says that an object has a certain property—that is, it is possessed of the power to manifest a sensible quality or affect an instrument. A statement is said to be true when the sentence used to make the statement is constructed in such a way and of such elements as are conventionally used to locate and individuate something where the subject actually is and to ascribe to it a property that it actually has. If someone asks, "Does your statement correspond to the facts?" we may reply, "I think so," or "yes, certainly." Normally we do not explicitly affirm the truth or falsity of the statements that we make. The word "true" typically is used to refer to the statements of others as we pass judgment on them. Confirming a statement involves both agreeing with the statement and lending our authority to it.... Phrases like "that's true" and "I know" suggest that the person who is employing them has corroborating reason to accept the statement as his own. If I make a statement and you confirm it, I can be displeased with you if that statement turns out to be false. A statement is true when it expresses adequately the arrangement of things to which attention has been drawn. There are demonstrative criteria through which our attention is drawn to the right place at the right time—that is, to the place in which we are supposed to be able to discover that such and such is the case. The consummation of looking for something is seeing or noticing it. Thus we must be ready with criteria of identification prior to our seeing and noticing. But I can see many things without noticing them. Should I recognize something that I am not particularly looking for, I must have somewhere in my conceptual equipment the criteria for identifying it. If I say, "this desk is made of walnut," pointing to the desk and saying "walnut" will not prove that walnut exists. The object signified must be of the right kind or be the individual intended. There must be recognitive criteria that are singled out by the act of demonstrative reference. The predicate of an existential statement must be capable of being understood in terms of the predicate appropriate to the thing said to exist. This presupposes some knowledge of actual structures.

Natural scientists in much of their theoretical activity are, in fact, trying to form a mental picture of the mechanisms of nature that are responsible for the phenomena they observe. The forming of a mental picture, in effect, is the making of models. Models may be sentential or iconic. A model may be nothing more than a tentative analogue for the real, but as yet unknown mechanism or structure. The model itself may be modeled on things we know or understand only imperfectly. When theory construction is successful, that which is presented as a model of an unknown mechanism in one generation may in another generation be seen to approximate the physical structure of the object in question. In the lifetime of our fathers, if not in our own lifetime, the molecular structure of a solid was a mere postulate, a crude analogue to represent what we thought ought to be the case on the basis of evidence at hand. Today an electron microscope can take directly interpretable pictures of atoms within solids. Now we can understand why some solids behave as insulators, others as semiconductors, and still others as metals. To use another example, with nuclear magnetic resonance imaging we are able to determine sodium or phosphorus concentrations in compounds such as fats and carbohydrates in the living tissues of the human body. Various nineteenth-century models of the cell and its components in the twentieth century turn out to be a close approximation of the postulated structure.

THE PRINCIPLE OF FINAL
CAUSALITY

In *Physics* II.3 and *Metaphysics* V.2, Aristotle offers his general account of the four causes. At the risk of oversimplification, Aristotle's doctrine of four causes may be regarded as little more than an elaboration of our common-sense conviction that change stands in need of explanation, or expressed in metaphysical terms, the conviction that not only being but being in act is intelligible.

The material cause is that out of which a thing is made; the formal cause is its determining principle—that which makes the thing to be what it is. The material and formal causes are intrinsic and constitute the essence or nature of the being in question. The efficient and final causes are extrinsic. The efficient (producing, making cause, or agent) is the primary source of change or rest. The final cause is the end or purpose (*telos*), i.e., that for which the sake of change is introduced. All four causes may enter into the explanation of something, but need not in every case. Aristotle uses the example of the eclipse of the moon, an event that does not call for an explanation by purpose or final cause. The same may be said of any event where the accidental intersection of two causal chains may have tragic effects. The accidental event is without purpose and in a sense is unintelligible. We call it a mishap. Any change, of course, must be the change of something (material cause) from something (privation in the material cause) to something else, the change being necessarily effected by some agent (efficient cause) whose action may be presumed to be of a characteristic sort and the product, a characteristic result (final cause).

A contrasting position on causality—call it the "mechanistic explanation" of change, one embraced by the empiricist or positivist—is one that admits of efficient and material causality, but denies the reality of final causality and, consequently, purpose in nature. That position follows logically from certain conclusions about the nature of substance. If what we call substance, as Locke maintained, is but a convenient way to designate a constellation of events or set of properties, and then we add to Locke's understanding of substance Hume's reduction of causality to mere sequence (i.e., contiguity in space and continuity in time), we have changed our understanding of the nature of scientific explanation. Kant, although heavily indebted to the British empiricists, does not rule out the notion of end or finality, but treats it a regulative idea, a guide to the conduct of inquiry rather than as a feature of nature. If substance is but that aspect of nature that interests us at the moment, if causality is reduced to description and prediction, and if the notion that there is purpose in nature is only a regulative idea, then the peripatetic notion of causality no longer serves to explain the common-sense quest for intelligibility. The question then becomes how to designate the relationship between one set of activities and another.

John Dewey, undoubtedly the most influential North American representative of the Locke/Hume/Kant point of view throughout most of the twentieth century, gives us an answer.

Having banished the notion of substance, once understood to be the subject of change, he substitutes the thesis that things are changes; change is simply a connected series of events, and causality is but another name for the sequential order itself.[1] To single out one part of the process and call it the cause of what follows is to act gratuitously. We may notice instances in which one event repeatedly follows another and may expect further instances of the same process, but so far such expecting is nothing but a useful habit. We do not know how long the habit will continue to be useful. To Dewey, then, causality is but another name for regular sequence. At most it enables us to expect that a certain event will follow upon another that precedes it, but in this there is no necessity. Our prediction will always lack certitude. The causal principle, in Dewey's analysis, is simply advice to look for regularities in natural processes.

It is to be admitted that the principle of repetition is a useful one in determining purpose. Both Aristotle[2] and Aquinas[3] assert that when things happen for the most part, that is, regularly, the *telos* of the activity is evident; e.g., birds build nests in the spring, squirrels bury nuts in the autumn, most fish regularly spawn in the spring and always spawn in the same habitat: water. An empiricist can admit regularity and yet deny that regularity can be explained. It is a feature of nature, to be sure. We can account for it in mechanistic terms without attributing purpose to the agents in question.

Causality, on a strictly empiricist analysis, becomes wholly subjective. If a relation on the part of things independent of the mind cannot be verified, the logical outcome of such a course is

1. John Dewey, *Logic: The Theory of Inquiry* (New York: Henry Holt, 1938), 127; Dewey, *Experience and Nature* (New York: W. W. Norton, 1929), 99.
2. Aristotle, *Physics*, II.8.198b–99a.
3. Thomas Aquinas, *Summa Contra Gentiles*, Bk II, ch. 86.

skepticism. Again, if causality is wholly a product of the mind imposing order on a chaotic universe, if there is no necessity in nature and no guarantee that the future state of things will resemble the past, all propositions become tentative or hypothetical. The innate compulsion of the mind to find regularity in nature overlooks many irregularities, so much so that the value of knowledge is rendered suspect.

Up to a point, the empiricist analysis of causality is correct. We do not experience necessity in nature. It is true, past experience leads us to expect certain events in the future, but it is difficult to avoid the question, "why?" The empiricist ably describes induction without explaining why induction is possible. One can grant that the senses report only a sequence of events. They do not report that one thing is the cause of another. What the empiricist fails to recognize is that there is more in the sense report than the senses themselves are able to appreciate; the resulting failure in effect reduces all knowledge to sense knowledge.

This account, we have maintained in previous lectures, is at variance with actual procedure in the sciences. To use one famous example: When Marie Curie began to study minerals, her attention was drawn to the mineral pitchblende uraninite. She reasoned that its emission of rays could only be explained by the presence in the ore of an unknown substance or substances. Joined by her husband, Pierre, she undertook to resolve the question. Using sophisticated measuring techniques, by measuring the action of the rays given off by magnetic fields, they proved the existence of varying amounts of three types of particles—electrically positive, negative, and neutral ones, particles that Sir Ernest Rutherford later called alpha, beta, and gamma rays. The varying amounts of the particles, it was eventually determined, were caused by the radioactivity of radium and thorium. The term "radioactive" was first used by Marie in 1898. The investigative techniques of the Curies in the same year led them to deduce the existence of two previously unknown elements, polonium (in honor of Marie's home country) and radium. Clearly their discoveries were not the product of an observed sequence. Rather, what we find here is a reasoned explanation for something otherwise unintelligible.

The explanatory principle involved in the Curie example is the principle of efficient causality. Expressed in its simplest form, this principle states that things or events that do not fully explain themselves with respect to their origins or properties must be explained in terms of something other than themselves. Mere experience of things joined in space and time is not enough. The question of why we experience things always conjoined begs to be answered. The fact that two things are always conjoined sequentially or by proximity may be due to the fact that they are causally related. Only through a reasoning process does the intellect grasp the causal bond. To call something the cause of the other is an attempt to explain the other. One is unintelligible without the other, as the chair is unintelligible without the carpenter, or growth without nutrition. Michelangelo is required to explain the marble statue of David, just as the moon is required to explain the movement of the tides.

To use another example, a child who has experienced a storm connects the blowing of the wind with the movement of the branches of the trees that are within sight. From experience he knows that the tree is alive and that living things are capable of self-motion, but knowing nothing of the source of the moving wind, he may reason that the lively movement of the tree is the source of the wind. He has instinctively sought intelligibility, although incorrectly identifying the cause of the wind. And yet another example of the instinctive search for intelligibility: Readers of the *Wall Street Journal* are daily confronted with reports similar to the following: "The Dow Jones Industrial Average plummeted by 376 points or nearly four percent to 10,068 in the stock market's latest fraught reaction to (fill in the blank)." No connection is ever demonstrated, yet the quest for an explanation is never absent in the editorial mind or in the mind of the public generally. A common reaction to the news is: "What happened?" Common sense is never satisfied with mere sequence.

Of Aristotle's four causes, the principle of final causality is the most troublesome for the empiricist or positivist. For Aristotle, a full explanation of anything must consider not only its efficient, material, and formal causes, but its final cause—the purpose for which the thing was designed or produced. Human conduct, insofar as it is rational, is usually explained with reference to ends pursued or alleged to be pursued, and human thought tends to explain the behavior of other things in nature on this analogy, either as pursuing ends or as a design to fulfill a purpose determined by a transcendent intelligence responsible for order in the cosmos. Modern science in the sixteenth and seventeenth centuries rightly shifted its interest to mechanistic explanations of natural phenomena, limiting explanation to efficient and material causes. It must be acknowledged that the endeavor to explain sensible things in the light of their substantial form or *telos* was a stumbling block in the Peripatetic tradition for centuries. Its sterile attempts were quickly outmoded by the quantitative procedures of modern physics and chemistry. Today we would say there is no point in asking the purpose of limestone deposits in Indiana or that of penguins in the Antarctic. Yet the question haunts: Can biological processes be explained in purely physicochemical terms? Does not the recognition of structure, function, and organization necessitate other than a mechanical explanation?

To admit purpose or design in nature is to admit a designer. For Plato it was a *demi-urgos* who introduced order into the chaotic flux of matter to produce a cosmos. Plato also acknowledged a *summum bonum* that draws all things to itself. Aristotle reasoned to both a first efficient cause and an ultimate final cause. From the *Phaedo* we learn that the study of nature consists in a search for the causes of each thing: why each thing comes into existence and why it exists. We do not have proper knowledge of a thing until we have knowledge of its cause. One may say that Aristotle conceives of causal investigation as a search for an answer to the question "why," and a "why" question is a request for an explanation. An adequate explanation of natural change may involve reference to all four causes, but not in every case.

Returning to *Physics* II.8, we find Aristotle's most general exposition of final causality. Aristotle was well aware of the objections to the principle of finality advanced by his contemporaries and subsequently carried through the centuries into modernity. Empedocles had put forward the theory that existing animal species, with all the adaptation of their parts to ends, are simply the result of natural selection by the survival of the fittest. Nature, Empedocles surmised, had produced an enormous variety of species, perhaps "cattle with men's faces" and the like, and that only the fittest survived.

In opposition to Empedocles, Aristotle tries to prove the existence of teleology in nature. Taking rain as an example, he acknowledges that rainfall may be for good or bad. It may happen that grain in the field is nourished or that the harvest is spoiled as a result of the rain. The good or bad result is a matter of coincidence. Cannot all natural change be accounted for in the same way? he asks. We can specify what brought the change about by identifying its efficient and material causes. In the case of rain, when warm air has been drawn up and is cooled off and becomes water, this water falls down as rain (*Physics* 198b.19–21). Can this not be a model for all supposed final-cause explanation? Aristotle will answer "no." The primary business of the natural philosopher is to state the form, definition, or end of the object of his inquiry. He does not always look for a final cause. Natural phenomena are due to simple and absolute necessity. They flow inevitably from the nature of the matter. The seasons follow each other. Rain follows from the formation of clouds. Animals breed to type. Sometimes this absolute necessity serves ends, but we must not always look for a final cause. Aristotle finds that the only events that are absolutely necessary are those that form part of a recurrent sequence or series. Variable characteristics or monstrous growths can be explained by material and efficient causes, and can be thought to serve no end. By necessity animals have eyes to see, but the color of the eyes is due to the conditions of birth and serves no end.

Reproduction has for Aristotle a special interest. The perpetuation of type is for him the clearest evidence of purpose in nature: "Whenever there is plainly some final end to which a motion attends should nothing stand in the way, we always say that such a final end is the aim of the motion; and from this it is evident that there must be something really existing, corresponding to what we call by the name of Nature. For a given germ (seed) does not give rise to any chance living being, nor spring from any chance one; but each germ springs from a definite parent and gives rise to definite progeny. And thus it is germ that is the ruling influence and fabricator of the offspring."[4]

Aristotle offers another example that shows the inadequacy of the coincidence explanation. It cannot be a mere coincidence that the front teeth grow sharp and suitable for tearing the food and the molars grow broad and useful for grinding the food. When the teeth grow this way, the animal survives. When they

4. Aristotle, *On the Parts of Animals*, 641.23–29, as quoted by W. D. Ross, *Aristotle: A Complete Exposition of His Works and Thought* (Cleveland: Meridian, 1959), 25.

do not, the animal dies. Can it reasonably be claimed that the way the teeth grow is not for the sake of the animal and its survival but a mere coincidence? Furthermore, this dental arrangement happens regularly, and where there is regularity there is a call for explanation. Coincidence is no explanation. To say that teeth grow as they do by material necessity and that this is good for the animal, by coincidence, is to leave unexplained the regular connection between the growth of the teeth and the needs of the animal. Aristotle argues that there is no way to explain organic development other than by reference to its end.

St. Thomas, addressing the issue, offers a metaphysical argument as follows: "Were an agent not to act for a definite effect, all effects would be indifferent to it. Now that which is indifferent to many effects does not produce one rather than another. Therefore, from that which is indifferent to either of two effects, no effect results unless (the agent) be determined by something to one of them. Thus it would be impossible for it to act. Therefore, every agent tends to some definite effect that is called its end."[5] This principle is often expressed by the Scholastic axiom, "There is no action without attraction." To Aquinas, an explanation in terms of a final cause is an attempt to render an action intelligible by giving its end or purpose, the reason the activity takes place. To deny the principle of finality is to deny that change is intelligible. Just as man's activity is unintelligible apart from its purpose, so too is all activity in nature unintelligible apart from its purpose. An explanation solely in terms of efficient cause is not satisfying. Plato had advanced a similar argument in the *Phaedo.* He puts into the mouth of Socrates a telling refutation of mechanism.[6] According to Socrates, in order to explain why he is

5. Aquinas, *Summa Contra Gentiles,* Bk. III, ch.2.
6. Plato, *Phaedo,* 98, in *The Dialogues of Plato,* translated by B. Jowett (New York: Random House, 1937).

sitting in prison, a mechanist can do no more than describe the physiological fact that his muscles and nerves and bones are related to each other in such a fashion that he is occupying a sitting position in this place. Such physiological principles, of course, are causes for the fact that Socrates is sitting in prison, but the most important cause for the imprisonment is overlooked. That cause is the purpose of his being where he is awaiting execution, something unaccounted for by a purely mechanistic explanation.

To approach the reality of final causality from another point of view: Where every natural agent of a particular type regularly produces one effect rather than another, some explanation is required. If the effect regularly produced is not actually intended—that is to say, if it is not the final cause of the agent's operation—then there is no sufficient reason it is regularly produced rather than some other effect. To deny the principle of finality is to deny that everything that occurs has a sufficient reason for its occurrence; it is to deny that things naturally tend to produce the effects that they regularly do produce. It is to deny, for example, that seeing is the natural end of the power of sight or hearing the power of hearing, to deny that eyes have any greater tendency to see than they have to hear. It is to make sight a mere accidental effect of the eyes. It is to say that the conjunction of eyes, colored objects, and light is a mere coincidence, and not a coincidence once, but every time we see. If it is admitted that natural agents do tend to certain effects, then they act for an end. Mechanical explanation will not suffice.

A positivist, Moritz Schlick, for example, may say that a teleological conception of nature, freed from its metaphysical and anthropological presuppositions, can still be held.[7] We can still speak of purposiveness, but without an anthropological notion

7. Moritz Schlick, *Philosophical Papers,* translated by Peter Heath, et al., edited by H. Muller and B. Van de Velde-Schlick (Dordrecht: D. Reidel, 1979), 1:xxxiii.

of purpose. Purposiveness, for Schlick, consists in the systemic interconnection of parts of a whole whose outcome, in spite of all sorts of outer and inner variations, is specific, and whose end result is largely predictable owing to the interlinkage of those parts.

One of the most conspicuous features of an Aristotelian view of the universe is Aristotle's thoroughgoing teleology. Yet modern interpreters of Aristotle such as Ross, Pichard, Cooper, and Hardie, while admitting that there is in nature an unconscious striving toward ends, are reluctant to say outright that the structure and history of the universe are the fulfillment of a divine plan. Time and again Aristotle says, "Nature does nothing in vain," and at least once says, "God and nature do nothing in vain." Ross thinks that when he uses the name "God," he is merely accommodating himself to common opinion.[8] Yet Alexander ascribed to Aristotle a belief in providential activity, and certainly the notion was not foreign to the thought of Socrates or Plato.

The notion of an unconscious teleology remains unsatisfactory for a number of reasons. It defies common sense. Our common experience of action is a teleological one; our intention is to reach our goal by our action. If we view action not merely as producing a result but as being aimed at the result, we must view the agent either as imaging the result and aiming at reaching it or as the tool or instrumental cause of some other intelligence that consciously aims at the result. Unconscious teleology implies a purpose that is not the purpose of any mind, and hence not a purpose at all.

An appeal to chance as an explanation of why certain things come about fails to explain order in nature. Chance itself can only be explained in terms of order. Where events repeatedly occur, we do not regard them as occurring by chance, but as or-

8. Ross, *Aristotle: A Complete Exposition*, 182.

dered. Aristotle makes this point when he concludes that the chance event is the intersection of causal series.[9] Likewise, any attempt to explain activity in terms of structure, accidentally or by chance acquired through an evolutionary process, will merely push the problem back one step further. The empiricist will still have to explain why this rather than that structure has emerged. Structure is only intelligible in terms of the purpose of the entity in question.

With the rise of modern science and its focus on material and efficient causality, final causes were simply eliminated from philosophical discourse, and with it any notion that there are natural obligatory ends with respect to human fulfillment. The implications for ethics are enormous. Any and all natural obligations, duties, or "oughts" disappear as well. No one has pointed this out more clearly than Henry Veatch in his *Aristotle: A Contemporary Appreciation.*[10]

9. Aristotle, *Physics* II, ch.5.

10. Henry Veatch, *Aristotle: A Contemporary Appreciation* (Bloomington, Ind.: Indiana University Press, 1974); see also Veatch, "Telos and Teleology in Aristotelian Ethics," in *Studies in Aristotle,* edited by Dominic O'Meara, 279–96 (Washington, D.C.: The Catholic University of America Press, 1974).

PART THREE

CULTURAL
CONSIDERATIONS

USE AND ABUSE OF ANALOGY AND METAPHOR IN SCIENTIFIC EXPLANATION

Aristotle observed that even the most abstract of thought is necessarily accompanied by a sensory image. This notion came to be expressed by the Scholastic dictum, "There can be no intellection without accompanying sensation." The function of images in scientific explanation will be addressed, but the immediate focus of this lecture is the use of metaphor in communicating insight into natural phenomena. Models employed in the sciences are a kind of metaphor in which a familiar structure or mechanism is used as an analogy to interpret natural phenomena.

Historians of science tell us that scientific models are often suggestive in the development of new theories and in the modification of existing ones. Niels Bøhr said of his own work that he could not understand anything unless he could make a model of it. In my school days, the Bøhr model of the atom was to be found in every science classroom. That model, of course, gave way as we learned more about atomic and subatomic structure. New models introduced us to electron orbits, quantum leaps, and similar constructs. Maritain complained in his *Philosophy of Nature* that in the domain of mathematical physics it is sometimes difficult to distinguish fact from theory. Pierre Gassendi, an early-seventeenth-century mathematician and philosopher, cautioned: "It is not permitted to transfer into Physics something abstractly demonstrated in Geometry," an admonition often forgotten. Myanna Lahsen, an anthropologist who spent several years interviewing staff at the National Center for Atmospheric Research, reports that a member of the staff once confided, "It is easy to get caught up in it: you start to believe that what happens in your model must be what happens in the real world. And often it is not true."[1] Yet even mathematical physics, though seemingly confined to the world of abstract necessity, must return to the empirical for confirmation. A physicist may formulate his findings in the language of laws and express these by means of equations, but he still thinks in terms of things that govern his work.

From an Aristotelian point of view, every scientific explanation is necessarily a realistic explanation, not a nominalistic one. Even Kant, who separated the world of logic from the ontological, assigned to metaphysics the role of preventing the employment of reason beyond its limits. He conceded: "*Intellectualia* as objects serve only as *modo cognoscendia* for the sensitive *dabilium*."[2] Theoretical physicists who have had some training in classical philosophy readily identify themselves as Aristotelians. Mathematical description, they acknowledge, is not scientific explanation.

Pursuing a point made above, it is clear that if the investigator himself sometimes fails to distinguish fact from theory, how much more difficult it is for the layman to do so. Popular accounts of scientific reports come laden with metaphor, often

1. *Wall Street Journal,* February 1, 2006, A-15.
2. Immanuel Kant, *Fragments,* 17:533, translated by Paul Bowman, edited by P. Guyer (Cambridge: Cambridge University Press, 2005), 13.

colorful, but not helpful. We are puzzled by the metaphor, "wrinkle in space time," and equally mystified when we hear someone speak of gravity as "warped space time." We read of "anti-matter," "drops of electricity," "black holes," "right- and left-handed spin of K-mesons," "backward causation," and "strong locality." And I haven't even mentioned "string theory." What, if anything, is conveyed to the layman by these terms? When the concept "anti-matter" was first introduced, the news was reported in ominous terms on the front page of major newspapers across the country. One of my classmates was called upon by a reporter for Washington's *Herald Tribune* for an explanation. The upshot was that a graduate student in physics at the Catholic University was depicted as having refuted a prominent physicist at Berkeley. Of course he had done no such thing; he was merely unpacking a simile or metaphor. My friend endured quite a bit of ribbing from his colleagues, but within little more than a decade, he became chairman of the physics department at a major research university. We know the mischief that can be created through the improper use of terms such as "evolution," "indeterminacy," and "relativity." In a given scientific community metaphor may be a shorthand way of referring to certain data, to a theory, or to a working insight. Thus, although a metaphor may have a meaning within a specific context, employed outside of a cognizant community, as, for example, when it is thrust upon a newspaper reader by a flamboyant reporter, it can be mystifyingly vague and convey no information at all. It is true that context confers meaning, but that is not the whole story. Our sympathy is with Alice when she confronts Humpty Dumpty, who insists that "words mean just what I want them to mean." As a good Aristotelian, Alice could have said that the meaning of a term is determined by its referent, the ontological structure to which it is applicable. Aristotle took it for granted that the way we think and talk about natural entities is, for the most part, the way they are, but he does not go so far as to suggest that language directly mirrors nature. Language certainly provides some indication of the structure of reality, but it can be a source of error.

Historians of science provide numerous accounts of how interesting metaphors enter the vocabulary of physics. Ernest Lord Rutherford, in proposing a mental model of the atom in 1911, drew an analogy between the solar system and the hydrogen atom. The nucleus of an atom, he found, is more massive than the electron, just as the sun is more massive than the planets. The nucleus attracts the electron in a relationship that causes the electron to revolve around the nucleus. A year later, Bøhr, utilizing information drawn from quantum mechanics, offered an alternative model in which he suggested that electron orbits were not like planetary ones; they were more like the rungs of a ladder, with electrons only at the rungs and not in between. Another famous example followed the calculation by Lisa Meitner and her nephew, Otto Frisch, based on a report by Strassmann and Hahn, that determined that the uranium nucleus had indeed been split. Frisch remembered that Niels Bøhr once remarked that the nucleus of an atom behaved something like a drop of liquid. With that metaphor in mind, Frisch asked one of his colleagues, a biologist, what biologists called the splitting of a cell. "Fission," came the reply, and the concept "nuclear fission" entered the common vocabulary.[3] Max Black, who has written at length on models and metaphors, saw a tight connection between the two, concluding that a model is nothing other than the explanation of a metaphor. Black was convinced that the first level of scientific activity, to the extent that it culminates in a hypothesis, begs to be complemented by an image. The image need not be concrete to be suggestive enough to

3. Cf. Ruth Moore, *Niels Bøhr: The Man, His Science, and the World They Changed* (Cambridge, Mass: MIT Press, 1985), 227.

guide research.[4] To use another example, this one offered by Giorgio de Santillana (in a passage entitled, "The Embarrassment of Reality"), who tells us that Maxwell's highly mathematical theory of gases assumed the reality of hard elastic particles. As de Santillana comments, "Real representations fight their way through progressive abstraction and the all-embracing theorems of physics and chemistry."[5] Theory begs to be complemented by the physical image. Metaphors can, of course, be inappropriate and misleading as well as suggestive. As a form of analogy, metaphor is the weakest form, lacking the clarity of proper proportionality and the force of analogy of attribution. In the natural sciences nothing can be proved by analogy, suggestive though some analogies may be. An egregious use of analogy is provided by a front-page article in the *New York Times* of April 6, 2006, entitled "Fossil Called Missing Link from Sea to Land Animals." The report tells us that the fossilized skeletal remains of a giant fish has features that anticipate the emergence of land animals and, in the words of the report, "is thus a predecessor of amphibians, reptiles and dinosaurs, mammals and eventually humans."[6] One can't argue with someone at that level of gratuitous confidence!

The poet can speak of "the yellow fog that rubs its back upon the window pane," and the metaphor is suggestive, conveying an image and creating a mood. The ancients referred to the "heaven of fixed stars" and spoke of the planets as "wanderers," descriptions that anyone who has spent a sleepless night under the stars

4. Max Black, *Models and Metaphors: Studies in Language and Philosophy* (Ithaca, N.Y.: Cornell University Press, 1962).

5. Giorgio de Santillana, *Reflections on Men and Ideas* (Cambridge, Mass.: MIT Press, 1968), 251.

6. The research was first published in *Nature,* by Erik Ahlberg of Uppsala University and Jennifer Clark of the University of Cambridge. The scientists offered their description of the forward fins of the 375-million-year-old fish as evidence of limbs-in-the-making. The fins, it is claimed, are the beginnings of digits, proto-wrists, elbows, and shoulders.

can appreciate. In a poetic mood, Copernicus spoke of the sun as "the lantern of the universe, at rest in the middle of everything ... for in this beautiful temple [the universe] who would place the lamp in another or better position than that from which it can light up the whole thing at the same time?"[7] We delight in the images conveyed and recognize their merit or their appropriateness, but the intellect remains aware that reality differs from that poetically suggested. Apart from its poetic value, metaphor as employed in the sciences can suggest or focus attention on reliably attained information or systematically acquired observation. Robert Sokolowski, writing from a phenomenological point of view, tells us, "Metaphors are enlightening precisely because they would be incoherent if taken literally. The fact that they don't literally fit what we are talking about makes us scrutinize the object more carefully than we have been accustomed to; we let it manifest itself in a new way."[8] Discussions of metaphor inevitably lead to deeper issues addressed in the philosophy of science.

Reflections on the nature and capacity of human knowledge did not await the eighteenth century or the advent of modern mathematical physics. Plato's discussion of science and claims to knowledge by the Greeks will forever remain the starting point of the philosophy of science. It was Plato who bequeathed to Western philosophy the insight that all science is of the universal. Aristotle concurred, finding the universal not in some unseen realm of archetypes, but in the nature common to members of a species. Aristotle taught that by a process of abstraction we come to know the essence, nature, or quiddity of a thing, prescinding from its accidental features, which it may or may not

---

7. As quoted by Fernand Hallyn, *The Poetic Structure of the World* (New York: Zone Books, 1995), 127.

8. Robert Sokolowski, *Husserlian Meditations: How Words Present Things* (Evanston, Ill.: Northwestern University Press, 1974).

have while remaining the thing that it is. Such is the object of science: a knowledge of the nature of things or the structure of a process as known from their properties and potentialities. Yet to have scientific knowledge is not simply to know what is, not simply to have uncovered a law of nature. For Aristotle to have scientific knowledge is to know the entity, process, or property in the light of its cause or causes. To have achieved a scientific explanation is to have rendered intelligible something that was not self-intelligible. The ancients, for example, knew well the properties of metals such as copper, gold, and silver, and they knew how to form alloys with them for specific purposes, but why those metals possessed certain properties and no others had to await the twentieth century. Why is copper malleable, a conductor of heat, a conductor of electricity, and relatively light in weight? Any attempt at explanation must first acknowledge that there is such a thing as copper, must recognize that "copper" is not a name we give to a bundle of properties, but a natural structure or substance, the source of those properties. For an empiricist such as Auguste Comte to advance theories concerning the why or what of phenomena is to commit a cardinal sin, the vice of a mind wholly alien to the true scientific spirit. Following the lead of David Hume, Comte would reduce science to description and prediction. Ever since the Pythagoreans, Western science has tended to view nature in purely mathematical terms. Galileo looked upon mathematics as the instrument by which man is enabled to understand the script God employed in creating the universe. Kepler shared this view when he wrote, "Just as the eye was made to see colors, the ear to hear sounds, so the human mind was made to understand Quantity."[9] But the natural sci-

9. Johannes Kepler, *Opera I,* 31, as quoted by Christopher Dawson, in *Progress and Religion* (Garden City, N.Y.: Doubleday, 1960).

ences consist in more than measurement, more than an account of quantitative relations and variations. It is true that much of the activity we associate with the natural sciences is indeed an attempt at description, an attempt to get straight the data or the facts under consideration. But the mind is not so easily content. It seeks to know the intrinsic nature of things, why things are as they are. Much of that knowledge is by inference. The knowledge we have of the submicroscopic, for example, is by inference. The mental mechanisms by which we hold that knowledge entail the creation of models, plausible mechanisms responsible for the phenomena observed. Models may be either sentential (an equation, for example) or iconic (a mental picture or a diagram). Thus in the history of theoretical physics, as our knowledge increases, we find successive schema depicting the atom. We are led to recognize that our knowledge of nature is open-ended, the focus of an intellectual quest that is never satisfied. In 1933, the state of particle physics was such that it seemed necessary to postulate the existence of a particle as yet undetected. As I mentioned in a previous lecture, the Italian physicist Enrico Fermi, assuming its existence, built his theory of beta decay upon it. The existence of the particle that Fermi has named "neutrino" was later empirically verified.

Analogy or metaphor sometimes plays a role when researchers trained in one area or in one method attempt to apply that method beyond its capacity. Emile Durkheim, Auguste Comte, and their American disciple, John Dewey, optimistically thought that if the method that had been successfully employed in the natural sciences were utilized in the sciences of man, we could expect there to be a similar success. Unavoidably, no matter how useful mathematical techniques may be in the study of nature, subject matter yet determines method. The way we ordinarily talk of mind and human agency does not fit well with our understanding of the world derived from the physical sciences. The realm of reason, the realm of judgment, of belief, and of desire are independent of physical facts about human agency. We may be every bit a part of nature, as are the inanimate elements that surround us, but there are facts about what we think and what we do that have no counterparts when the subject is a plant or animal. To explain human behavior in the language of physics or chemistry, or by causal accounts that cast human beings as a collection of physical particles, is to miss that which is distinctive about human beings.

A frequent mistake in this area of research is to confuse mind with brain activity, assuming that the nervous system and the brain are the cause of what goes on in "consciousness." From an Aristotelian point of view, mind is clearly bodily, and as such cannot be discussed apart from brain activity. Discussions of the intellect are something else. While intellection cannot take place apart from sensation, the two are not the same. How one discusses the relationship depends first on a clear distinction between sensation and intellection. Sense knowledge provides the material for the intellectual formation of concepts that transcend sensory experience. Yet there is more in the sensory report than the senses themselves are able to appreciate. Recognition of the transcendent or nonmaterial aspects of human knowing entails a modeling of human nature that finds a prototype in Aristotle, in contrast to reductionist accounts that ignore or falsify data in the interest of simplicity.

Perhaps the most serious consequence of a failure to understand the nature of scientific explanation is what may be called a "failure of misplaced expectations." The notion of progress, taken for granted in physics, chemistry, and biology, cannot be predicated of the sciences that depend on our knowledge of human nature, what Charles Taylor calls "the sciences of man."

Christopher Dawson makes the case that "faith in progress" is one of the most dangerous ideas to find its way into modernity. No one can fail to notice that there is a certain linear progression in our knowledge of nature, cumulative and ever more precise, enabling its application to achieve feats undreamt of even in a previous generation. With respect to our knowledge of human nature, such progress does not exist. This holds consequences for the social and political sphere. Whereas our knowledge of nature increases almost day by day, there is no similar increase in our knowledge of human nature. True, we know more about the human body and its functioning than was known even in the last century, let alone in ancient times, but knowledge of the human body is not the same as a knowledge of human nature. There is a difference between mathematical description and mechanical explanation, on the one hand, and philosophical reflection, on the other. The natural sciences advance on the back of technology and are directly traceable to the use of instruments—i.e., telescopes, microscopes, particle accelerators, and other specialized investigative tools—but there are no instruments available today that were not available in antiquity when the subject is human nature. Governments may have the technical resources to explore the solar system, but those same governments cannot with confidence set out to eradicate poverty, improve education, or devise immigration policy without taking into account certain time-transcending facts about human nature. In setting norms for collective action, policy makers must resort to a higher order of learning—namely, that wisdom that finds its source in the classics of Western culture, sources identified with the work of Plato, Aristotle, the Stoics, Augustine, Boethius, the fathers of the church, and their commentators through the ages.

SCIENCE AND THE
SHAPING OF MODERNITY

THE RECIPROCAL INFLUENCE
OF SCIENCE AND CULTURE

Cultural historians necessarily deal in broad generalizations. Whatever is affirmed of a period, a people, or a nation, no matter how well grounded by factual study and reflection, is subject to qualification. Exceptions to broad characterizations may always be found without mitigating the value of the broader insight. We grasp something when an author refers to the Greeks, to Roman civilization, to the Hellenic period, to Christendom, to the Benedictines, to the Renaissance, or to the Enlightenment. These designations, all generalizations formed by an examination of a host of particulars, indeed refer to something intelligible, something quite apart from the mind.[1] Generalization, of course, can be

---

1. Lynn White, Jr., reminds us of the Herculean task awaiting the cultural historian. He writes, "History is being made faster than we can absorb it.... As yet no mind, not even Arnold Toynbee's, has really digested the new material"; White, "The Changing Past," in *Frontiers of Knowledge in the Study of Man,* edited by Lynn White, Jr., 68 (New York: Greenwood, 1969).

misleading or false as well as perceptive and true. There is always the danger of unscrupulous forces manipulating history for present purposes. Then, too, in the study of history there is always the propensity to judge the past in the light of contemporary categories of experience. It is axiomatic that one must banish from the mind the customary conceptions of one's own period before one can rightly understand the past. With that caveat in mind, this essay purports to examine, with the aid of a host of distinguished twentieth-century scholars, the reciprocal influence of science and culture with particular attention to the role of religion at the birth of modern science.

Detached narrative is rare, yet, for example, those acquainted with the lifelong work and studied objectivity of Christopher Dawson are likely to give credence to his insight when he speaks of the great movement of thought that passed over the ancient world about the middle of the first millennium B.C. "that turned away men's minds from the world of human experience to the contemplation of absolute and unchanging Being, from Time to Eternity."[2] There are few readers who are in a position to render the same judgment unaided. Similarly, Dawson is convincing when he writes that with the advent of Christ, "the Absolute and the Finite, God and the World were no longer conceived as two exclusive and opposed orders of being standing over and against one another in mutual isolation. The two orders interpenetrated one another."[3] Dawson's judgment is an invitation to reflection. He makes a like generalization about the advent of modern science and its medieval antecedents. Scholars are nearly unanimous in recognizing that something dramatic occurred in the culture of Europe around the turn of the eleventh century. Explanations

2. Christopher Dawson, *Progress and Religion* (Garden City, N.Y.: Doubleday, 1960), 123.
3. Dawson, *Progress and Religion*, 126–27.

vary, with some emphasizing technological advancement, others the recovery of Greek learning, still others the practical influence of Christianity.

In 1925 the distinguished American philosopher Alfred North Whitehead delivered the prestigious Lowell Lectures at Harvard University, lectures subsequently published as *Science and the Modern World*.[4] Those lectures were significant because Whitehead, for a predominately American audience, challenged the Enlightenment view that only with the repudiation of a religious world view could modern science have emerged from a dark age. Whitehead, it must be noted, was writing a generation before the in-depth studies of Marshall Clagett, A. C. Crombie, and Anneliese Maier, and before the monumental work of Pierre Duhem became available in English translation. Examining the relation between science and culture, Whitehead put to himself a fundamental question: "Why did modern science emerge in the West during the sixteenth and seventeenth centuries when all the conditions required for its birth were seemingly in place in classical antiquity?" That question has entered public consciousness again with the reemergence of militant Islam. Contemporary scholars, in their attempt to understand an adversarial Islam, ask why the scientific revolution that we associate with Europe bypassed Islam, when for centuries Islam was in many respects at the forefront of human civilization and achievement. Bernard Lewis, the noted Middle East scholar, pointedly asks, what went wrong?[5] He writes, "In the course of the twentieth century it became abundantly clear in the Middle East and indeed all over the lands of Islam that things had indeed gone badly wrong. Compared with its millennial rival, Christendom, the world of Islam had become

4. Alfred North Whitehead, *Science and the Modern World* (New York: Macmillan, 1925; 4th ed. New York: Mentor, 1953).
5. Bernard Lewis, *What Went Wrong?* (Oxford: Oxford University Press, 2002).

poor, weak, and ignorant."[6] "Why," he asks in a subsequent passage, "did the great scientific breakthrough occur in Europe and not as one might reasonably have expected in the richer, more advanced, and in many respects more enlightened realm of Islam?"[7]

Putting aside for the moment Lewis's somewhat romantic view of the "Golden Age of Islam," his question has been addressed, perhaps never more authoritatively, by A. C. Crombie.[8] In the same vein, a more recent account of the development of modern science, one that we will subsequently discuss, is that of Stephen Gaukroger.[9] Crombie's research led him to the conclusion that the new science that began to percolate into Western Christendom in the twelfth century, although largely Arabic in form, was founded on the works of the ancient Greeks. The Arabs, Crombie relates, preserved and transmitted to medieval Europe a large body of Greek learning, adding to it to be sure, but what they added to its content was perhaps less important than the change they made in the conception and purpose for which science ought to be studied. The speculative or theoretical aspect of science interested them less than its application. In the judgment of Crombie, the most important and original contributions that the Arabs made to the history of European science were those of alchemy, magic, and astrology. This was due partly to the Arabic approach to the study of nature, where power over nature, rather than rational explanation of fact, led inquirers to seek "the Elixir of Life," the magic properties of plants and minerals, instead of the causes of the properties of the things they experienced.[10]

6. Lewis, *What Went Wrong?* 151.   7. Lewis, *What Went Wrong?* 156.

8. A. C. Crombie, *Medieval and Early Modern Science,* vol 1, *Science in the Middle Ages: V–XIII Centuries;* vol. 2, *Science in the Later Middle Ages and Early Modern Times: XIII–XVII Centuries* (Garden City, New York: Doubleday Anchor, 1959).

9. Stephen Gaukroger, *The Emergence of a Scientific Culture: Science and the Shaping of Modernity, 1210–1685* (Oxford: Clarendon Press, 2006).

10. Crombie, *Medieval and Early Modern Science,* 1:52.

It has been well documented that the Arabs themselves acquired their knowledge of Greek science from two sources: initially from Syriac intermediaries, but later directly from the Greeks of the Byzantine Empire. Their first encounter with Greek learning came from the Syriac-speaking Nestorian Christians of Eastern Persia.[11] The role that the Arabs played in the transmission of Aristotle to the West is an interesting and complicated story in itself and cannot be recounted here, but this much needs to be said: with the rapid expansion of Islam after Muhammad's death in 632, regions where Greek learning had previously been deposited came under Islamic domination. Under the Abbasid caliphs after 749, Muslims established contact with both Christians and Hellenized Persians. The Abbasid caliphs and other patrons of translating activity were primarily interested in works of immediate practical utility—i.e., technical treatises on medicine, astrology, logic, and the mathematical sciences.[12] "Partly through the growth of scholastic theology," David Lindberg tells us, "Islamic interests quickly expanded to encompass the whole of Platonic and Aristotelian philosophy. Texts already available in Syriac, the language of the Nestorian Christian community, were translated into the Arabic. Works not available in Syriac were rendered directly from Greek into Arabic."[13] The high-water mark of translations from Arabic to Latin came during the twelfth century. Lindbergh finds that the story of the transmissions of Greek learning to the West

11. Cf. David C. Lindberg, "The Transmission of Greek and Arabic Learning to the West," in *Science in the Middle Ages,* edited by David C. Lindberg, 55–56 (Chicago: University of Chicago University Press, 1978).

12. Lindberg, "Transmission of Greek and Arabic Learning," 56. For an alternative account, one written from an Islamic perspective, see George Saliba, *Islamic Science and the Making of the European Renaissance* (Cambridge, Mass.: MIT Press, 2007). Saliba confirms with considerable textual evidence Crombie's account of the westward transmission of astronomical data from the world of Islam and makes the case that Copernicus's heliocentric view of the universe was largely indebted to Arab sources.

13. Lindberg, "Transmission of Greek and Arabic Learning," 56.

is largely a tale of individual scholars responding in personal ways to unique historical circumstances. Yet there were important centers, such as Toledo and Palermo, where significant, if not cooperative, work was being done. In 1250, for example, the provincial chapter of the Dominicans in Toledo sent eight friars to the *studium arabicum* in Tunis. By that time the works of Aristotle were diffused and understood throughout the Latin West. Interest in Aristotle was accompanied by interest in the philosophical works of the great speculative thinkers al Kindi, al-Farabi, and Avicenna, all Persians. The most influential Arabic thinker of the period was undoubtedly Averroes (1126–1198), who was regarded as the interpreter of Aristotle par excellence and was frequently referred to simply as the "Commentator."

Perhaps the better focus, unlike that of Lewis, should be not upon what went wrong in Arabia, but what went right within Christendom. Whitehead provides this insight: "My explanation is that the faith in the possibility of science, generated antecedently in the development of modern scientific theory, is the unconscious derivative from medieval theology."[14] "The Middle Ages," Whitehead claims, "formed one long training of the intellect in Western Europe in the sense of order. There may have been some deficiency with respect to practice. But the idea never for a moment lost its grip. It was predominantly an epoch of orderly thought, rationalistic through and through."[15] Yet for science, something more is necessary than a general sense of the order of things. Equally important is the habit of definite and exact thought, which Whitehead attributes to the Greek philosophers, a legacy carried through the Middle Ages. Whitehead in this passage is less interested in the metaphysics that undergirds induction than he is in the impact of technological advance and

14. Whitehead, *Science and the Modern World,* 14.
15. Whitehead, *Science and the Modern World,* 12.

the reciprocal influence of the theoretical and the practical. "We owe to St. Benedict," he writes, "that the monasteries were the homes of practical agriculturalists, as well as saints, and artists and men of learning. The alliance of science and technology, by which learning is kept in contact with irreducible and stubborn facts, owes much to the practical bent of the early Benedictines. Modern science derives from Rome as well as from Greece and this Roman strain explains its gain in an energy of thought kept closely in contact with the world of facts."[16]

The medieval historian Lynn White, Jr. later develops this theme in an article entitled "The Dynamo and the Virgin Reconsidered." Like Whitehead he calls attention to the significant role that the Benedictines played in the history of Western technology, saying of St. Benedict that he was probably "the pivotal figure in the history of labor."[17] White, in comparing the status of labor in ancient Greece with its status in the later Middle Ages, finds that in the classical tradition there is scarcely a hint of the dignity of labor. The civilizations of ancient Greece and Rome had rested on the backs of slaves. Reversing this Greek attitude toward labor was St. Benedict, by making labor part of the corporate life of his monastery, by adopting it not merely as a regrettable necessity, but rather as an integral and spiritually valuable part of monastic discipline. White suggests that the Benedictine regard for the dignity of labor "marks a revolutionary reversal of the traditional attitude to labor: it is the high peak along the watershed separating the modern and ancient world." Moreover, although St. Benedict had not intended that his monks should be scholars, a great tradition of learning developed in the abbeys following his *Rule:* for the first time the practical and the theoretical

16. Whitehead, *Science and the Modern World,* 16.
17. Lynn White, Jr., "The Dynamo and the Virgin Reconsidered," *American Scholar* 27 (1958): 187.

were involved in the same individual. "The monk," White continues, "was the first intellectual to get dirt under his fingernails. He did not immediately launch into scientific investigation, but in his very person he destroyed the old artificial barrier between the empirical and the speculative, the manual and the liberal arts, and thus helped to create a social atmosphere favorable to scientific and technological development."[18]

What Whitehead dimly saw, Crombie makes explicit in his well-documented *Medieval and Early Modern Science,* a history of science from Augustine to Galileo, from its decay after the collapse of the Roman Empire in the West to its full flowering in the seventeenth century.[19] He emphasizes what he believes are the two most significant results of twentieth-century scholarship: the essential continuity of Western scientific traditions from Greek time to our own and the significance of medieval discussions of scientific methodology. Crombie's wide study has convinced him that the most significant changes in the history of science are always brought about by new conceptions of scientific procedure. It is Crombie's thesis that if modern science owes most of its success to the use of inductive and experimental procedure, then it owes a great deal to the philosophers of the thirteenth and fourteenth centuries who first produced an understanding of that experimental procedure. He credits them with transforming the Greek geometrical method into the experimental science of the modern era. Although the conception of scientific explanation accepted by Galileo, Harvey, and Newton is a theory of formal proof developed by Greek geometers and logicians, the distinctive feature of the seventeenth century, Crombie writes, is non-Greek in origin. It is a scientific method based on "a conception of how to relate a theory to observed facts it explained, the set of logical

18. White, "The Dynamo and the Virgin Reconsidered," 188–89.
19. Crombie, *Medieval and Early Modern Science.*

procedures ... for constructing theories and for submitting them to experimental tests."[20] Whereas Aristotle distinguished natural science on the basis of subject matter, deriving three orders of abstraction—physics, mathematics, and metaphysics—the medieval mind tended to look upon this distinction as not one of subject matter, but method of inquiry. The philosophers of the thirteenth century distinguished clearly among the kinds of questions to be asked under each level of inquiry. Crombie likens this to the role of linguistic analysis in our own time. The object of the experimental method worked out during this period was to discover and define the conditions necessary and sufficient to uncover the experiential data. It was recognized that a theory defining these conditions could never be certain: it was necessary to "save the appearance," but it may not be "necessarily true" in the sense of being a *demonstrated* conclusion. The effect of this tendency to regard mathematics as a method rather than a domain or province of study was to change the kind of questions asked. Interest gradually shifted from the physical or metaphysical to the kind of question that could be answered by a mathematical theory within reach of experimental verification. The history of medieval science shifts to the working out of the consequences of this new approach to nature. Examples of this shift are seen in the sciences of statics, optics, and astronomy.[21]

Crombie is not alone in his view. Whitehead and Dawson imply as much.[22] Lynn Thorndike[23] and W. C. Bark[24] take similar views. Dawson makes much the same point when he compares

20. Crombie, *Robert Grosseteste and the Origins of Experimental Science, 1100–1700* (Oxford: Oxford University Press, 1971), 1.
21. Crombie, *Robert Grosseteste,* 2–3.
22. Whitehead, *Science and the Modern World,* 12.
23. Lynn Thorndike, *A History of Magic and Experimental Science,* 8 vols. (New York: Columbia University Press, 1923–58).
24. See especially W. C. Bark, *Origins of the Medieval World* (New York: Doubleday Anchor, 1960), 115 ff.

the utilitarian view of science propounded by Roger Bacon in the fourteenth century with the speculative view of science entertained by the Greek mind. Bacon is obviously closer to the modern mind than to the Greek when he makes science an instrument of world conquest and exploitation. Dawson suggests that both the utilitarian view and the Greek view of science contributed to the European scientific tradition: "The pragmatic experimentation of the Baconian ideal could have borne no fruit apart from the intellectual training and discipline which were provided by Aristotelian scholasticism."[25]

Other scholarship suggests that it is from Robert Grosseteste that Bacon derived his distinctive philosophical and scientific views.[26] Both Dawson and Crombie accord him a major role in the history of scientific theory, using Grosseteste as a symbol of the fusion of two traditions. Crombie writes: "From the almost pure empiricism of such practical sciences of the twelfth century as practical mathematics, astronomy, and medicine, and the almost pure rationalism of theoretical speculation in contemporary philosophy on scientific method, he [Grosseteste] produced a science in which he tried to show the principles according to which the world of experience could be experimentally investigated and rationally explained."[27] Other important elements of Grosseteste's thought are his conception of physical nature, in which the essence or "form" is mathematically determined, and his conception of the immediate objective of inquiry as mathematical and predictive laws instead of Aristotelian essential definition. These concepts, Crombie maintains, were not without their effect, for

25. Christopher Dawson, "Origins of European Scientific Tradition," *The Clergy Review* 2 (1931): 203.

26. Cf. Pearl Kibre and Nancy Sirasi, "The Institutional Setting of the Universities," in *Science and the Middle Ages,* edited by David C. Lindbergh, 128–29 (Chicago: University of Chicago Press, 1978).

27. Crombie, *Robert Grosseteste,* 43.

in the fourteenth century we find developments of mathematical technique designed to take advantage of the new methodology and conceptions of explanation. At the same time, extension of the use of experiment and mathematical abstraction had begun to produce results so striking that this movement in itself could well be called a "scientific revolution."

Benjamin Farrington similarly attributes the success of Renaissance science to the technological revolution of the Middle Ages.[28] According to Farrington, when the classic works arrived in the West, the West was prepared. Medieval man had learned the use of natural resources and upon this had built a society in which humans were free from a large part of their former drudgery. Technical advance had led to social change. The slave had been replaced by the serf and the craftsman.[29] Concerning the relation of the new technology to slavery there are a number of theses. Lynn White, who has directed considerable attention to the subject, suggests that the development of medieval technology owes its impetus to the Christian teaching of the infinite worth of the individual and the church's opposition to slavery. In his article "Dynamo and Virgin Reconsidered" White notes that whereas Henry Adams can symbolize an age by the concept of "dynamo," the early Middle Ages can be characterized by the devotion shown to Our Lady: "St. Bernard's Cistercian monks were so devoted to the Virgin that every one of their hundreds of monasteries was dedicated to her; yet these White Benedictines seem often to have led the way in the use of power."[30] In a seminal article entitled "Technology and Invention in the Middle Ages," White argues: "The chief glory of the later Middle Ages was not its cathedrals or its epics or its scholasticism: it was the building

28. Benjamin Farrington, *Greek Science* (London: Penguin, 1952), 307ff.
29. Farrington, *Greek Science*.
30. White, "The Dynamo and the Virgin Reconsidered," 190.

for the first time in history of a complex civilization which rested not on the backs of sweating slaves or coolies but primarily on non-human power." The laborsaving power machines of the later Middle Ages were produced by the implicit theological assumptions of the infinite worth of even the most degraded personality, by the intrinsic repugnance toward subjecting any man to monotonous drudgery that seems less human, in that it requires the exercise neither of intelligence nor choice. It has often been remarked that the Latin Middle Ages first discovered the dignity and spiritual value of labor—that to labor is to pray. But the Middle Ages went further; they gradually and very slowly began to explore the practical implications of an essentially Christian paradox: that "just as the heavenly Jerusalem contains no temple, so the goal of labor is to end labor."[31] In defending this thesis, White is developing Lefebvre des Noëttes's argument that the new inventions destroyed slavery by making it unnecessary and undesirable.[32] On the other hand, the French medieval historian Marc Bloch has argued that the end of slavery came first and created a necessity to which such devices as the new harness and water mill were the response.[33] Both Crombie and Bark nevertheless defend the view that the church, although it never succeeded in completely stamping out slavery, was greatly aided in its opposition to slavery by the new laborsaving devices.

31. White, "Technology and Invention in the Middle Ages," *Speculum* 15 (1940): 156.

32. The medieval contribution to technology gained recognition as a result of the researches of Commandant Lefebvre des Noëttes, a one-time cavalry officer, who upon retirement from military life turned his professional attention to account by making a historical study of animal power. This work, published in the early 1930s, eventually led him to accumulate an impressive body of evidence on medieval technical developments and their social consequences. The result of his work has been praised as one of the capital historical discoveries of the early twentieth century; cf. des Noëttes, *l'Attelage et le cheval de selle à travers les ages* (Paris: 1931); des Noëttes, *De la marine antique à la marine moderne* (Paris: 1935).

33. Cf. Marc Bloch, *Feudal Society,* translated by L. A. Manyon (Chicago: University of Chicago Press, 1961).

In the opinion of Pierre Duhem (1861–1916), author of the classic ten-volume history of the physical sciences from Plato to Copernicus, *Le Systeme du monde*,[34] if we had to assign a date to the birth of modern science, we would be compelled to choose the year 1277, when Étienne Tempier, Bishop of Paris, solemnly condemned 219 philosophical and theological propositions then currently entertained within the Arts Faculty and the Faculty of Theology of the University of Paris. His example was followed in the same year by the Archbishop of Canterbury, John Pecham. From the vantage point of Duhem, it was significant that the condemnations undermined the authority of Aristotle insofar as they condemned the Peripatetic theory of place and everything that Aristotle's *Physics* asserted about infinity, place, and time and the possibility of a void.

It is to be remembered that Aristotle arrived in Paris with considerable baggage—imperfect translations, to be sure, but more damaging were the often misleading commentaries of Averroes. Of the 219 theses condemned by Tempier, many were Averroistic in nature. Although no names were mentioned in the condemnations,[35] many were presumably held by Siger of Brabant and Boethius of Dacia. Some of the condemned theses were held by Albertus Magnus and Thomas Aquinas. Just how many of them were clearly Thomistic depends, Gilson remarks, on whether the list "is compiled by a Franciscan or a Domini-

34. Pierre Duhem, *Le Systeme du monde: Histoire des doctrines cosmologiques de Platon à Copernic* (Paris: Hermann, éditeurs des sciences et des arts, 1954). Selections from Duhem's massive work have been translated and made available by Roger Ariew, *Medieval Cosmology: Theories of Infinity, Place, Time, Void, and Plurality of Worlds* (Chicago: University of Chicago Press, 1985); cf. also Stanley Jaki, *Uneasy Genius: The Life and Work of Pierre Duhem* (Dordrecht: Martinus Nijhoff, 1984).

35. For an authoritative account of the condemnation, cf. John F. Wippel, "The Condemnations of 1270 and 1277 in Paris," *Journal of Medieval and Renaissance Studies* 7 (1977): 169–201; see also Wippel, "Thomas Aquinas and the Condemnation of 1277," *Modern Schoolman* 72 (1995): 233–72.

can."[36] William A. Wallace provides a cautionary note when he writes, "It is generally agreed that Duhem's thesis is extreme, for there is no indication of a spurt in scientific thought or activity following 1277, and it is doubtful whether any authoritarian restriction on cosmological teachings could have stimulated that free spirit of inquiry that is generally seen as characteristic of modern science."[37] Yet Wallace concedes, "It is undeniable that the condemnation of 1277 had an effect on the development of medieval science, although not as profound as was maintained by Pierre Duhem."[38] Clearly the condemnation did not seriously affect the study of Aristotle. With Albert and Thomas, scholars began to sort out what in Aristotle was merely outmoded science or cosmology from the time-transcendent value of his philosophy of nature and its supporting metaphysics. It is not an exaggeration to claim that Aristotle's philosophy of science remains viable in the twentieth century. Whereas Gilson speaks of the 1277 condemnation as a "landmark," Stephen Gaukroger employs the notion of a "paradigm shift" to suggest the magnitude of the change.

The investigation of the physical world or natural philosophy, until the thirteenth century, was regarded as part of a single philosophical activity. Its purpose was to discover the enduring and intelligible reality behind the changes perceived though the senses. With the condemnation of the deterministic (Averroistic) view of Aristotle, the authority of Aristotle was challenged, thus undermining confidence in his entire system. In the judgment of Crombie, the natural philosophers of the thirteenth century,

36. Étienne Gilson, *History of Christian Philosophy in the Middle Ages* (New York: Random House, 1955), 728.

37. William A. Wallace, "Philosophical Setting of Medieval Science," in *Science in the Middle Ages,* edited by David C. Lindberg, 105–6 (Chicago: University of Chicago Press, 1978).

38. Wallace, "Philosophical Setting of Medieval Science," 105.

"because of the skepticism of Christian theologians," were freed from the authority of Aristotle and thus free to develop the empirical habit of mind, but within a rational framework.[39]

Cultural historians agree that since classical antiquity there have been a number of civilizations that have witnessed a scientific revolution. Stephen Gaukroger,[40] whose work we will now consider, speaks of the "rich productive scientific cultures, in which fundamental and especially intractable, physical, medical, astronomical, and other problems are opened up and dealt with in an innovative and concerted fashion, producing cumulative results over several generations."[41] Besides Greece and the Hellenic diaspora, he identifies these as the Arab/Islamic North Africa/Near East/Iberian Peninsula in the ninth, tenth, and eleventh centuries, Paris and Oxford in the thirteenth and fourteenth centuries, and China from the twelfth to the fourteenth century.[42] The scientific revolution of seventeenth- and eighteenth-century Europe is something different, he thinks, insofar as the uninterrupted and cumulative growth of the early modern period breaks with the boom/bust pattern of earlier cultures. Not only that, but the scientific revolution was so spectacular that it not only displaced competing accounts, but was extrapolated to all cognitive disciplines. In a relatively short period of time, Copernicanism and Darwinism came to replace firmly held philosophical and theological views concerning nature and the order in nature that had persisted since biblical times.

39. Crombie, *Medieval and Early Modern Science,* 1:64.

40. Graukroger is writing some eighty years after Whitehead and fifty years after Crombie. Specialized studies subsequently written abound, yet the basic facts as well as most interpretations remain unchanged; cf. Stephen Gaukroger, *The Emergence of a Scientific Culture: Science and the Shaping of Modernity, 1210–1685* (Oxford: Clarendon Press, 2006).

41. Gaukroger, *The Emergence of a Scientific Culture,* 17.

42. Graukroger, *The Emergence of a Scientific Culture,* 18.

Stephen Gaukroger, like Whitehead, takes exception to what he calls the "Enlightenment interpretation"—namely, that the scientific revolution occurred as a result of Western science's ability to disassociate itself from religion. Vigorously challenging that "self-serving account," he writes: "Far from science breaking free of religion in the early modern era, its consolidation depended crucially on religion being in the driver's seat: Christianity took over natural philosophy in the seventeenth century, setting its agenda and projecting it forward in a way quite different from that of any other scientific culture."[43] Gaukroger's strong claim is defended in what promises to be a multi-volume study, the first of which is entitled, *The Emergence of a Scientific Culture: Science and the Shaping of Modernity, 1210–1685.*

In demonstrating the continuity of science and technology through the later Middle Ages into modernity, Gaukroger contrasts the progress of science in the West with that in the cultures of Islam and China. "Arab-Islamic science," he writes, "had two distinctive features. The first is that there was no institutional support available for scientific work that was not motivated by extra-scientific concerns.... Second, the way in which the achievements of Greek philosophers, and Greek and Alexandrian mathematicians, were 'naturalized' in the Arab-Islamic culture is distinctive. They were domesticated, incorporated into an indigenous culture and philosophical system, rather than being institutionalized in such a way that they carried 'their own specific gravity of autonomy and legitimacy, independent of the moral and religious scruples of the surrounding culture.' The consequence of these two institutional features of Arab-Islamic civilization is that while it was occasionally possible for innovations to be made in astronomy, optics, and even metaphysics,

43. Gaukroger, *The Emergence of a Scientific Culture*, 23.

there was no way in which they could be followed up in a systematic manner."[44]

With respect to China, the situation was almost the reverse. "If Arabic-Islamic culture could initiate scientific developments but not follow them up, China had an extensive network of communication, and this acted in such a way as to foster scientific and technological achievement. In the Sung and Ming dynasties we find inventions such as mechanical clocks, moveable type, and seismographs that predate developments in the West by a couple of centuries, and we find significant advances in observational astronomy and medicine."[45] Yet there were serious obstacles to innovation that were not practically oriented. The bureaucratic structure of Chinese society was a crucial factor. Then, too, traditions of philosophical disputation are relatively marginal in Chinese intellectual culture. Adherence to tradition plays a crucial role in all artistic and intellectual pursuits, with the result that there was a strong sense that scholarship rather than innovation is the path to wisdom. This was reinforced by the Confucian tendency to self-effacement and avoidance of contentiousness, as well as a strong commitment to outward obedience to public authorities. This Chinese respect for authority formed a sharp contrast with Greek models of confrontational debate.[46]

Crombie's study is reinforced by Gaukroger when he writes that, "In the thirteenth century, philosophy was transformed from a marginal enterprise into one that was to provide the principal point of entry into understanding of the natural world and our place in it."[47] The engine of transformation was Aristotle's natural philosophy in spite of the condemnations. Gaukroger

44. Gaukroger, *The Emergence of a Scientific Culture,* 33.
45. Gaukroger, *The Emergence of a Scientific Culture,* 33.
46. Gaukroger, *The Emergence of a Scientific Culture,* 33.
47. Gaukroger, *The Emergence of a Scientific Culture,* 33.

thinks the significant event is not Étienne Tempier's condemnation of 1277, but the much earlier Paris condemnation of Aristotle in the year 1210. He uses that date as a starting point as he traces the development of natural philosophy from the Scholasticism of the early thirteenth century, through the corpuscularism and atomism associated with Gassendi and Mersenne, to Descartes' cosmology and to Hobbes's mechanism. The year 1685 Gaukroger uses to mark the twilight, if not the demise, of Aristotelian natural philosophy and the ascendancy of a period dominated by the works of Locke, Newton, and Leibniz. He maintains that from the thirteenth to the fifteenth century two models had provided the unity of knowledge: one was the Aristotelian notion of *scientia,* the other the Christian idea of a universe designed and created *ex nihilo* by a single God as an abode for human beings. In the seventeenth century both were confronted by nominalistic and mechanistic interpretations of nature. Copernicus was thought to displace a man-centered universe, Darwin to displace *Genesis,* and Hobbes's mechanism to displace the recognition of design in nature.

The shift from an Aristotelian worldview to modernity, although gradual, was radical. Pagan philosophers had made natural philosophy the basis of moral philosophy. Aristotelian categories had been employed by the early church fathers as they interpreted the texts of the Gospel. Justin Martyr, Marius Victorinus, and Clement of Alexandria recognized that Aristotelian natural philosophy, while not intrinsically Christian, was nevertheless not inherently pagan. Aristotelian natural philosophy, although not without rivals, notably those of the neo-Platonic and Augustinian schools, held sway until it gave ground to mechanistic interpretations of nature in the seventeenth century, notably that advanced by Pierre Gassendi (1592–1655). It is Descartes and his artificially created "mind-body problem" that stimulated Gassendi to address the age-old problem of universals and the relation between sense and intellectual knowledge.[48] In his criticism of Descartes, he writes, "When you say that you are simply a thing that thinks, you mention an operation that everyone was aware of but you say nothing about the substance carrying out this operation: What sort of substance it is, what it consists in, how it organizes itself in order to carry out its different functions."[49] Gassendi's atomism in its pre-Newtonian form is an attempt to explain macroscopic phenomena by means of the microscopic. Presented as a matter theory inspired by the Greek atomists, when combined with the doctrine of primary and secondary qualities, it undermined the Aristotelian concept of "nature" and, with it, teleology. But those implications and others are not what he intended. It is a small step from Gassendi's atomism to Auguste Comte's positivism.

Science in the Aristotelian sense, and above all an acknowl-edgment of its Scholastic roots, suffers greatly at the hands of Renaissance humanists. A number of scholars are of the opin-ion that the fifteenth-century humanism that arose in Italy and spread northward was an interruption of the development of sci-ence. The so-called revival of letters deflected interest from con-tent to literary style, and in turning back to classical antiquity, many humanists affected to ignore the progress of the previous three centuries. Unaware of how much they owed to their im-mediate predecessors, these humanists, by their contempt of Scholasticism, did much to initiate the Dark Age myth that the *philosophes* of the French Enlightenment were happy to perpetu-ate. Crombie suggests that "The same absurd conceit that led the humanists to abuse and misrepresent their immediate predeces-sors for using Latin constructions unknown to Cicero and to put

48. Cf. the excellent study of Antonia Lolordo, *Pierre Gassendi and the Birth of Early Modern Philosophy* (Cambridge: Cambridge University Press, 2006).
49. As quoted by Lolordo, *Pierre Gassendi,* 228.

out the propaganda, which in varying degrees has captivated historical opinion until quite recently, also allowed them to borrow from Scholasticism without acknowledgment. The habit affected almost all the great scientists of the sixteenth and seventeenth centuries, whether Protestant or Catholic, and it has required the labors of Duhem and Maier to show that their statements on matters of history cannot be accepted at face value."[50]

Whitehead is convinced that the natural scientists of the sixteenth and seventeenth centuries were anti-intellectualists in the same way as the religious reformers were anti-intellectualists.[51] Herbert Butterfield recalls how the humanists of the Renaissance, Erasmus included, were accustomed to complaining of the boredom of Scholastic lectures and suggests that this was due to the ignorance of the humanists more than anything else.[52] The humanists derided their Scholastic teachers, but these despised Scholastic disciplines now hold a remarkable key position in the story of the evolution of the modern mind. Butterfield writes: "Perhaps the lack of mathematics or the failure to think of mathematical ways of formulating things was partly responsible for what appeared to be verbal subtleties and an excessive straining of language in these men who were yearning to find the key to the modern science of mechanics."[53]

The Renaissance attitude took hold and has held sway since. For complex reasons, positivism has come to be associated with modern science. Positivism, insofar as it restricts knowledge to that attained by physico-mathematical methods, in effect reduces science to description and prediction. With remarkable insight,

50. Crombie, *Augustine to Galileo* (Melbourne: Heinemann, 1952), 268–69; cf. also Charles B. Schmitt's extended treatment, *Aristotle and the Renaissance* (Cambridge, Mass.: Harvard University Press, 1983).

51. Whitehead, *Science in the Modern World*, 12.

52. Herbert Butterfield, *Origins of Modern Science* (New York: Macmillan, 1957), 2.

53. Butterfield, *Origins of Modern Science*, 2.

Christopher Dawson, writing three-quarters of a century ago, commented, "The disease of modern civilization lies neither in science nor in machinery but in the false philosophy with which they have been associated.... Though these ideas accompanied the rise of the machine order, they are in reality profoundly inconsistent with that order and with scientific genius."[54] Elsewhere he remarks that "we cannot be sure that the world which science has made will be as favorable to the production of scientific genius as the world that made science."[55]

Karl Popper likewise indicts the positivistic attitude toward science in which the emphasis is placed on description and practical results. "Instrumentalism," Popper maintains, "is unable to account for the importance to pure science of severely testing even the most remote implications of its theories since it is unable to account for the pure scientist's interest in truth and falsity. In contrast to the highly critical attitude requisite in the pure scientist, the attitude of instrumentalism (like that of applied science) is one of complacency at the success of application. Thus it may well be responsible for the recent stagnation in theoretical physics."[56]

We did not begin with Bernard Lewis's question of what went wrong in the Islamic world, but shifted the discourse to what went right within Christendom. As contemporary Europe struggles with its identity, Dawson's work is there to remind us: "Europe is not a group of people held together by a common type of material culture; it is a spiritual society that owes its existence to the religious tradition which for a thousand years molded the beliefs, the ideals, and the institutions of European peoples."[57]

54. Dawson, *Christianity and the New Age* (London: Sheed and Ward, 1931), 102.

55. Dawson, *The Modern Dilemma* (London: Sheed and Ward, 1933), 49.

56. Karl Popper, *Contemporary British Philosophy* (New York: Macmillan, 1960), 381.

57. Dawson, *Progress and Religion,* 173.

Dawson adds a frightening thought: "If modern Europe falls either through internal revolution or through loss of her world leadership, modern civilization falls with her. For that civilization was entirely a European creation, and there is no force outside Europe to-day capable of carrying on her work, whatever the case a century or two hence."[58]

58. Dawson, *Progress and Religion,* 171.

EPILOGUE

These lectures, apart from their focus on the nature of scientific explanation, have shown through the use of history that science has a cultural dimension, both in its creation and in its use. Modern science is distinctly European and could have arisen only within a distinctive intellectual tradition centuries in the making. As to its cultural impact, many of the names we associate with the history of science were not oblivious to the social implications of the philosophy that ruled the day. F. A. Hayek saw this clearly when he wrote *The Road to Serfdom*.[1] Known primarily as an economist, he was also a philosopher of science. Like Karl Popper, Michael Polonyi, and Otto Neurath, he was interested in how those methods that had proven so successful in the natural sciences might be utilized in the sciences of man. Hayek was interested not so much in social policy per se as he was in the methodology that might be employed in the pursuit of a viable social policy. He believed that the positivism associated with the Vienna Circle led directly to a dangerous socialism.

For centuries Western Europe had commonly acknowledged that there is a will superior to the collective will of man and that there is an immutable law to which civil authority must bow. Positivism, by limiting knowledge to description and prediction, ruled out key metaphysical concepts such as "nature" and "pur-

---

1. F. A. Hayek, *The Road to Serfdom* (Chicago: University of Chicago Press, 1944).

pose in nature," thus preventing an appeal to a time-transcending moral order. Absent a teleological conception of nature, a skeptic may rightly ask, "how can one move from a description of what is to what ought to be?" Once justice, understood as one of Plato's cardinal virtues—being a metaphysical concept based on an acknowledgment of a natural order—is discarded as empirically worthless, justice must be redefined. Similarly, freedom no longer means what from a classical point of view it was thought to mean. Traditionally it meant that a man could not be compelled to do anything contrary to reason and conscience. Limited to positive knowledge, freedom came to mean that a man could not be compelled to do anything except by law enacted in accordance with some prescribed procedure with sufficient force behind it to compel obedience. From the positivist's standpoint, what was once called rights became merely concessions granted by the state or society. Hayek recognized that if rights are the product of law, they are not properly rights at all; they are mere concessions to claims that the individual makes and the state recognizes. As such they can be withdrawn if the state deems such withdrawal in the interest of the general welfare. Viewed from the perspective of positivism, the rights of man are no longer to be regarded as "natural rights"; they are mere "legal rights."

Hayek was convinced when he wrote *The Road to Serfdom* that positivism tended to divide political theorists into left and right wings. Writing while the outcome of World War II was still uncertain, he called attention to the fact that the socialist policies endorsed by the "progressive intellectuals" of the day are the same as those of the 1920s and 1930s that gave Europe National Socialism. *The Road to Serfdom* may be fruitfully read as a historical review of the social and economic policies that prevailed in Europe during the first decades of the twentieth century, but that was not Hayek's primary purpose in writing the book. It was issued as a prophetic warning, yet as Hayek modestly writes, "one does not have to be a prophet to be aware of impending disaster.... When one hears for the second time opinions expressed and measures advocated which one has met twenty years ago, they assume a new meaning as symptoms of a definite trend: they suggest the probability that future developments will take a similar turn." He continues, "It is necessary now to state the unpalpable truth that it is Germany whose fate we are in danger of repeating. This danger is not immediate, it is true, and conditions in England and the United States are still so remote from those we have witnessed in Germany as to make it difficult to believe we are moving in the same direction."[2] Still, he fears that the socialist policies endorsed by our progressive intellectuals will inevitably take their toll.

Hayek was not alone in his analysis of the past or in recognizing the danger that the emerging socialist parties posed for the future of Europe. Writing in France during the same period, Bertrand de Jouvenel produced a similar diagnosis of the events that brought the European dictators to power.[3] De Jouvenel's study of power and its acquisition serves as a lasting reminder that it is in the pursuit of utopia that the aggrandizers of power find their most effective ally, for only an immensely powerful apparatus can do all that the preachers of panacea government promise. Hayek, for his part, was much more engaged than de Jouvenel in the debate on economic planning that included Ludwig von Mises, Joseph Schumpeter, and Walter Schiff as well as Neurath, Polanyi, and Popper mentioned above.

Distancing himself from socialist planning, Hayek provided his own perspective on how a market economy is actually driven. In doing so he makes an important epistemological point. Most

2. Hayek, *The Road to Serfdom*, 377.

3. Bertrand de Jouvenel, *On Power: Its Nature and the History of Its Growth*, translated by J. F. Huntington (New York: Viking Press, 1945).

of the knowledge necessary for running an economic system, he holds, is not in the form of scientific knowledge—that is, by a conscious allusion to the principles governing natural and social phenomena. More important is the knowledge that may be described as intuitive and prudential in character—idiosyncratic knowledge consisting of dispersed bits of information and understanding relative to time and place. This tacit knowledge, which an Aristotelian would recognize as abstraction, is often not consciously possessed by those who make use of it and is of such a nature that it can never be communicated to a central authority. The market tends to use this tacit knowledge, as do individuals pursuing their own ends.

Ludwig von Mises had made a similar point in a 1920 article entitled, "Economic Calculation in the Socialist Commonwealth," wherein he wrote: "In the absence of a capitalist market, production costs and commodity values could not be determined. A central planning board could neither measure costs nor determine prices. Prices reflect not inherent but changing human preferences; they provide producers and distributors necessary information for planning production and distribution.... It is precisely in dealings that market prices are formed, taken as the basis of calculations for all kinds of goods and labor. Where there is no free market, there is no pricing mechanism; without a pricing mechanism, there is no economic calculation."[4] Both von Mises and Hayek insist that it is impossible to have any information, strictly speaking, without a pricing mechanism. Such information can only come from a free market. The centralized planning assumes a kind of geometric, a priori deductive knowledge on the part of the planners. A free market allows empirical truth to come to light. A good example of a free market is the real estate market.

4. Ludwig von Mises, "Economic Calculation in the Socialist Commonwealth," in *Collectivist Economic Planning,* edited by F.A. Hayek, 111 (London: Routledge, 1935).

The government cannot tell a person what he should be paying for a house, but socialism thinks it can do so.

Karl Popper, like Hayek, was a student of von Mises and was from the start a critic of the Vienna Circle, although in his early years Popper could be described as a heterodox socialist. Popper was badly shaken on reading *The Road to Serfdom,* Malachi Hacohen tells us in his biography of Popper.[5] In a letter to Hayek, Popper called it "one of the most important political books I have ever seen." To another correspondent, he wrote, "Hayek has seen very much sharper than I have that socialism leads directly to totalitarianism."[6] Popper in his autobiography discloses that he would have remained a socialist had he not begun to see that socialism put liberty at risk. In Hacohen's judgment, it was the massive support for fascism on the Continent that gave him pause. Popper came to the conclusion that "the paradox of democracy was real; if the majority were sovereign, then it could decide that it no longer desired a democratic government. It could, as a third of the German electorate did, vote the fascists into power."[7]

Socialism, considered abstractly, Hayek concedes, may not inexorably lead to totalitarian rule, but he is convinced that experience shows that the unforeseen and inevitable consequences of social planning create a state of affairs in which, if its policies are pursued, totalitarian forces will eventually get the upper hand. Ironically, he suggests, socialism can be put into practice only by methods of which socialists disapprove. *The Road to Serfdom,* Hayek reminds his reader more than once, was written in an effort to alert readers to the seemingly unstoppable trend in Western democracies to subject their national economies to central planning that unavoidably leads to tyranny. Even a strong tradi-

5. Malachi H. Hacohen, *Karl Popper: The Formative Years: 1902–1945* (Cambridge: Cambridge University Press, 2001), 485.

6. Hacohen, *Karl Popper,* 485.   7. Hacohen, *Karl Popper,* 507.

tion of political liberty, Hayek warns, is no safeguard. The democratic statesman who from the loftiest of motives sets out to plan economic life will soon be confronted with the alternative of assuming dictatorial power or abandoning his plans. In short order he will have to choose between disregarding ordinary morals and failure. Hayek is convinced that the unscrupulous and uninhibited, lacking the principles to constrain their activity, are most likely to assume positions of authority. Under their leadership, the moral views that initially inspired the collectivist state are not likely to prevail. The general demand for quick and determined government action will lead to a new morality and the suppression of democratic procedures. Given dissatisfaction with the slow and cumbersome course of constitutional procedures, the man or party that appears the strongest or seems the most resolute in getting things done is the one that will set the moral tone.[8]

Hayek is convinced that in a planned society it is not merely a question of what the majority of people agree upon, but what the largest single group or best-organized group agrees upon. It takes such a core group to make a unified direction possible. Such a group, Hayek believes, is not likely to be comprised of the best informed and most disinterested elements of society. In general the higher the education and intelligence of individuals, the more their tastes will differ and the less likely they are to agree on a set of ideas. "If we wish to find a high degree of uniformity and similarity of outlook, we have to descend to the regions of

8. Charles de Koninck addresses a third factor not specifically addressed by von Hayek when he identifies two kinds of "Master State": one motivated by totalitarian principles, the other by consumerism. For a discussion of de Koninck's position and the threat of social control posed by free enterprise, see Louis Groarke, *The Good Rebel: Understanding Freedom and Morality* (Fairleigh Dickenson University Press, 2002), 236–39. Groarke, like de Koninck, speaks of the insidious effects of consumerism. "Advertising," he wrote, "is used to create superfluous needs that can never be satisfied. The forces of marketing manipulate individuals, changing their outlook on life, orienting their behaviour, and in general inciting social conformity" (237).

moral and intellectual standards where the more primitive and 'common instincts' and truths prevail."[9]

It is worth remembering that both Hayek and Popper, though universally recognized as social theorists, were primarily focused on epistemological issues normally encountered in the philosophy of science. In fact when Hayek was appointed to the Committee on Social Thought at the University of Chicago, he offered a faculty seminar of the philosophy of science that was attended by some of the most notable scientists of the time, including Enrico Fermi, Sewell Wright, and Leo Szilard. Hayek, it must be noted, took the "old moral order," the inherited, for granted. Though under attack since the Enlightenment, it remained the cornerstone of European culture. He neither probed its sources nor defended it principles. John Dewey, by contrast, deliberately set out to challenge the inherited and through his voluminous writing prepared the way for socialism in North America; given his influence in China, many think he prepared the way for the cultural revolution of Mao Tse Tung. For Dewey the function of education is to challenge the inherited, to question the received—in effect, to take the measure of civilization in the light of the empiricism that we have associated with Hume, Comte, and the Vienna Circle. Implemented to the full, Dewey's progressive education deprives the student of those time-transcending truths about nature and human fulfillment to be found in the Greek poets, in Livy, Horace, Virgil, and Homer and in the texts of Plato, Aristotle, and the Stoics, not to mention their medieval commentators.

Before Kant and the contract theory of Thomas Hobbes, the natural moral law outlook of Aristotle and the Stoics was common academic fare. That teaching, following the lead of the English model, formed the basis of moral teaching in the early days of the American republic. The classical curriculum of the early

9. Hacohen, *Karl Popper,* 507.

American college, the curriculum that prevailed during the seventeenth and eighteenth centuries, concentrated on training students in the Seven Liberal Arts, a curriculum that can be traced through the Middle Ages to antiquity. Aristotle is prominently represented in the curriculum, along with Plato and the more philosophical works of Cicero. The classical curriculum remained in place throughout the eighteenth century. It was the curriculum that shaped the thought of the founders of the American republic. John Adams, in his defense of the proposed U.S. Constitution, quotes Aristotle in support of a "mixed constitution," one that he, Adams, recommended for its checks and balances.

Extraordinary advances in the natural sciences introduced a wealth of technical and specialized disciplines that often usurped the time given to classical studies. A counter trend in the twentieth century produced numerous efforts to revitalize the liberal education of the earlier period. The University of Chicago, under the tenure of its president, Robert M. Hutchins, introduced the Great Books movement in the early decades of the twentieth century. It was Hutchins's ambition to create a college curriculum based on the study of the great authors of the Western world from biblical times to the modern world. Aided by the editors of Everyman's Library and the Modern Library, the movement caught on, and one of the consequences was a renewed interest in classical learning. Richard McKeon, dean of the college under Hutchins, edited a widely used collection, *The Basic Works of Aristotle*.[10] Mortimer Adler, another Hutchins appointee at Chicago, edited with Charles Van Doren his own multi-volume collection, *The Great Books of the Western World*. Similar efforts to promote classical philosophy, notably the realism of Aristotle, are to be found in the mid-decades under the leadership of

10. Richard McKeon, ed., *The Basic Works of Aristotle* (New York: Random House, 1941).

John Wild at Yale University and John Herman Randall, Jr., and Mark Van Doren at Columbia. Classicists like John Burnet and A.E. Taylor were not without influence, but in spite of some success, the trend toward specialized education to the neglect of the liberal component has continued unabated.

Allan Bloom, in his 1987 book, *The Closing of the American Mind*,[11] describes the loss of educational standards in the 1960s, exemplified, he held, by the abandonment of the traditional core curriculum, the decline in the study of languages, both ancient and modern, and, significantly, the disappearance of "the King's English." He speaks of "the collapse of the entire educational structure, recognized by all parties when they talk about the need to go back to basics." The breakdown of standards and the repudiation of tradition are directly traceable, he believes, to both the teachings and the deeds of universities in the sixties. It may take some future historian to identify fully the causes and to explain how we entered what has come to be called the "terrible sixties," but Bloom offers a compelling insight. One is struck by his claim that the greatest thoughts and political principles exemplified in our founding documents became the exclusive province of our universities. Those principles, he believes, never became embodied in a living, self-perpetuating class of men. "Neither aristocrats nor priests, the natural bearers of high intellectual tradition, exist in any meaningful sense in America."[12] Since the home in America of those founding principles has been the universities, the violation of that home, Bloom holds, became the crime of the sixties. Tradition once broken, he reminds us, is not easy to recover: "one cannot jump on and off tradition like a train." Bloom ends his book on a pessimistic tone, convinced that it will not be easy to

11. Allan Bloom, *The Closing of the American Mind* (New York: Simon and Schuster, 1987).

12. Bloom, *The Closing of the American Mind*.

recover the knowledge of philosophy, history, and literature that was trashed in the sixties. The need for a liberally educated public he makes apparent. When education is organized on wholly utilitarian lines, Bloom tells us, we are deprived of a broadly educated class that possesses the wisdom, speculative and practical, to deal with contingencies in the light of the time-honored wisdom of the race. As the West is challenged by a self-confident and militant Islam, the value of a liberal education may come to be recognized, if for no other reason than the need to define the distinctive features of Western culture. Without a knowledge of the great thinkers of the past, it is impossible to understand who we are as citizens of the West, let alone how its culture came to be. Historians tell us that in periods of cultural decline, generations have resorted to classical learning to set things right. Edmund Husserl, speaking of Europe in the first decades of the twentieth century in his 1935 lecture "Philosophy and the Crisis of European Humanity," offered an analysis of Europe's spiritual and intellectual crisis that looked to ancient Greece as a way out of the crisis facing the West. Husserl found in the Greek spirit of philosophical inquiry the sources for "free and universal reflection that would serve as a model for a supra-national ideal of reason." In Husserl's words, "There are only two escapes from the crisis of European existence: the downfall of Europe and its estrangement from its own rational sense of life, its fall into hostility toward the spiritual, into barbarity; or the rebirth of Europe from the spirit of philosophy through a heroism of reason that overcomes naturalism once and for all."[13]

Clearly ours is not the first generation to look for a remedy in the face of cultural decline. Cicero, writing in the first century before Christ and addressing a troubled time when men felt that

13. Edmund Husserl, "Philosophy and the Crisis of European Humanity," in *The Crisis of European Sciences and the Transcendental Phenomenology,* translated by David Carr, 299 (Evanston, Ill.: Northwestern University Press, 1970).

the Roman state had declined, laid out the conditions of leadership. In Book V of *On the Commonwealth,* he speaks of inherited standards that "brought forth distinguished men, eminent men who cherished the ways and customs of our ancestors." Cicero was convinced that he who would rule ought to be a man of consummate ability and learning. In addition to his understanding of law, a governor must have studied Greek to gain access to Athenian philosophy. Cicero himself acknowledges a debt to Plato.

The core curriculum alluded to above was common to America's colleges through the 1950s. Its loss has resulted in a largely uneducated media and political class, whose lack of an intellectual and moral compass has affected the culture of the nation. Indeed, a question raised on both sides of the Atlantic is whether Western civilization can survive without being reanchored to its sources. If an intellectual and political class, for whatever reason, repudiates or ignores the Hellenic and Christian sources of Western culture, can European civilization survive? Charles A. Murray, in promoting his book *Human Accomplishment,* commented, "I write at a time when Europe's run appears to be over. Bleaker yet, there is reason to wonder whether European culture as we have known it will exist even at the end of this century."[14]

Nearly a century ago, Oswald Spengler, following Nietzsche, sounded the alarm that culture is not something abiding. One does not have to subscribe to Spengler's cyclical view of history or to Murray's recent assessment to recognize that something is amiss. The Enlightenment project to secularize Europe has taken its toll, not only in Europe, but wherever European culture has heretofore flourished. The question remains, given the amorphous state of our politicized universities: is it possible to reclaim the Hellenic and Christian sources of European culture?

14. Charles A. Murray, *Human Accomplishment: The Pursuit of Excellence in Arts and Sciences, 800 B.C. to 1950* (New York: Harper Collins, 2003).

BIBLIOGRAPHY

Aquinas, Thomas. *Summa Theologiae.* Translated by the Fathers of the English Dominican Province as *Summa Theologica.* 3 vols. New York: Benzinger Brothers, 1947.

———. *De Ente et Essentia.* Translated by Armand Maurer as *Being and Essence.* Toronto: Pontifical Institute of Medieval Studies, 1949.

———. *Summa Contra Gentiles.* Translated by Anton C. Pegis as *On the Truth of the Catholic Faith.* 5 vols. Garden City, N.Y.: Hanover House, 1955–1956.

Ariew, Roger. *Medieval Cosmology: Theories of Infinity, Place, Time, Void, and Plurality of Worlds.* Chicago: University of Chicago Press, 1985.

Aristotle. *Metaphysics.* Translated by W. D. Ross. In *Basic Works of Aristotle,* edited by Richard McKeon. New York: Random House, 1941.

———. *Physics.* Translated by R. F. Hardie and R. K. Gaye. In *Basic Works of Aristotle,* edited by Richard McKeon. New York: Random House, 1941.

Armstrong, D. M. "What Is a Law of Nature?" Cambridge: Cambridge University Press, 1983.

Black, Max. *Models and Metaphors: Studies in Language and Philosophy.* Ithaca, N.Y.: Cornell University Press, 1962.

Bark, W. C. *Origins of the Medieval World.* New York: Doubleday Anchor, 1960.

Bloch, Marc. *Feudal Society.* Translated by L. A. Manyon. Chicago: University of Chicago Press, 1961.

Bloom, Allan. *The Closing of the American Mind.* New York: Simon and Schuster, 1987.

Butterfield, Herbert. *Origins of Modern Science.* New York: Macmillan, 1957.

Crombie, A. C. *Augustine to Galileo.* Melbourne: W. Heinemann, 1952.

———. *Medieval and Early Modern Science.* Vol. 1, *Science in the Middle Ages: V–XIII Centuries.* Vol. 2, *Science in the Later Middle Ages and Early*

Modern Times: XIII–XVII Centuries. Garden City, New York: Doubleday Anchor, 1959.

————. *Robert Grosseteste and the Origins of Experimental Science, 1100–1700.*
Oxford: Oxford University Press, 1971.

Dawson, Christopher. *Christianity and the New Age.* London: Sheed and
Ward, 1931.

————. "Origins of European Scientific Tradition." *The Clergy Review* (1931):
203–24.

————. *The Modern Dilemma.* London: Sheed and Ward, 1933.

————. *Progress and Religion.* Garden City, N.Y.: Doubleday, 1960.

De Hass, Frans, and Jaap Mansfield. *Aristotle on Generation and Corruption.*
Oxford: Clarendon Press, 2004.

De Jouvenel, Bertrand. *On Power: Its Nature and the History of Its Growth.*
Translated by J. F. Huntington. New York: Viking Press, 1945.

De Santillana, Giorgio. *Reflections on Men and Ideas.* Cambridge, Mass.:
MIT Press, 1968.

Dewey, John. *Experience and Nature.* New York: W. W. Norton, 1929.

————. *Logic: The Theory of Inquiry.* New York: Henry Holt, 1938.

Duhem, Pierre. *Selections.* Translated from *Le Systeme du Monde,* translated
and edited by Roger Ariew. In *Medieval Cosmology, Theories of Infinity,
Place, Time, Void and Plurality of Worlds.* Chicago: University of Chicago Press, 1985.

Ellis, Brian. *The Metaphysics of Scientific Realism.* Montreal: McGill-Queens
University Press, 2009.

Farrington, Benjamin. *Greek Science.* London: Penguin, 1952.

Gaukroger, Stephen. *The Emergence of a Scientific Culture: Science and the
Shaping of Modernity, 1210–1685.* Oxford: Clarendon Press, 2006.

Gerson, Lloyd. *Aristotle and Other Platonists.* Ithaca, N.Y.: Cornell University
Press, 2005.

Gilson, Étienne. *History of Christian Philosophy in the Middle Ages.* New
York: Random House, 1955.

Groarke, Louis. *The Good Rebel: Understanding Freedom and Morality.* Fairleigh Dickenson University Press, 2002.

————. *An Aristotelian Account of Induction.* Montreal: McGill-Queens University Press, 2009.

Grossman, Reinhardt. *The Categorial Structure of the World.* Bloomington:
Indiana University Press, 1983.

Guicciardini, Niccolò. *Isaac Newton on Mathematical Certainty and Method.* Cambridge, Mass.: MIT Press, 2009.

Hacking, Ian. *Representing and Intervening.* Cambridge: Cambridge University Press, 1983.

Hacohen, Malachi H. *Karl Popper: The Formative Years: 1902–1945.* Cambridge: Cambridge University Press, 2001.

Hallyn, Fernand. *The Poetic Structure of the World.* New York: Zone Books, 1995.

Harré, Rom. *The Principles of Scientific Thinking.* Chicago: University of Chicago Press, 1970.

Harré, Rom, and E. H. Madden. *Causal Powers: A Theory of Natural Necessity.* Totowa, N.J.: Rowan and Littlefield, 1975.

Hart, Charles A. *Thomistic Metaphysics.* Englewood Cliffs, N.J.: Prentice-Hall, 1959.

Hayek, F. A. *The Road to Serfdom.* Chicago: University of Chicago Press, 1944.

Hume, David. *Inquiry Concerning Human Understanding.* Edited, with an introduction by Charles W. Hendel. New York: Macmillan, 1988.

Husserl, Edmund. "Philosophy and the Crisis of European Humanity." In *The Crisis of European Sciences and the Transcendental Phenomenology,* translated by David Carr, 269–300. Evanston, Ill.: Northwestern University Press, 1970.

Jaki, Stanley. *Uneasy Genius: The Life and Work of Pierre Duhem.* Dordrecht: Martinus Nijhoff, 1984.

James, William. *Varieties of Religious Experience.* London: Longmans, Green, 1902.

Jones, Shellia. *The Quantum Ten: A Story of Passion, Tragedy, Ambition, and Science.* Oxford: Oxford University Press, 2008.

Joseph, H. W. G. *Logic.* Oxford: Clarendon Press, 1906.

Kant, Immanuel. *Fragments.* Translated by Paul Bowman. Edited by P. Guyer. Cambridge: Cambridge University Press, 2005.

Kass, Leon. *Life, Liberty and the Defense of Dignity.* New York: Encounter Books, 2002.

Kibre, Pearl, and Nancy Sirasi. "The Institutional Setting of the Universities." In *Science and the Middle Ages,* edited by David C. Lindbergh, 128–29. Chicago: University of Chicago Press, 1978.

Lolordo, Antonia. *Pierre Gassendi and the Birth of Early Modern Philosophy.* Cambridge: Cambridge University Press, 2006.

Lewis, Bernard. *What Went Wrong?* Oxford: Oxford University Press, 2002.

Lindberg, David C., ed. *Science in the Middle Ages.* Chicago: University of Chicago Press, 1978.

Manicas, Peter. *A Realist Philosophy of Science: Explanation and Understanding.* Cambridge: Cambridge University Press, 2006.

Maritain, Jacques. *An Introduction to Philosophy.* Translated from the French by E. I. Watkin. New York: Sheed and Ward, 1937.

———. *Formal Logic.* Translated by Imelda Choquette. New York: Sheed and Ward, 1937.

———. *The Degrees of Knowledge.* Translated from the fourth French edition by Gerald B. Phelan. New York: Charles Scribner's Sons, 1959.

McIntyre, Alasdair. *Whose Justice, Which Rationality.* South Bend, Ind.: University of Notre Dame Press, 1988.

McKeon, Richard, ed. *The Basic Works of Aristotle.* New York: Random House, 1941.

Miller, Fred D. *Nature, Justice and Rights in Aristotle's Politics.* Oxford: Clarendon Press, 1997.

Moore, Ruth. *Niels Bøhr: The Man, His Science, and the World They Changed.* Cambridge, Mass.: MIT Press, 1985.

Murray, Charles A. *Human Accomplishment: The Pursuit of Excellence in Arts and Sciences, 800 B.C. to 1950.* New York: Harper Collins, 2003.

O'Meara, Dominic, ed. *Studies in Aristotle.* Washington, D.C.: The Catholic University of America Press, 1974.

Owens, Joseph. *The Doctrine of Being in Aristotelian Metaphysics.* Toronto: Pontifical Institute of Medieval Studies, 1957.

———. *Aristotle: The Collected Papers of Joseph Owens.* Edited by John R. Caton. Albany: State University of New York Press, 1981.

Plato. *The Dialogues of Plato.* Translated by B. Jowett. New York: Random House, 1937.

Popper, Karl. *Contemporary British Philosophy.* New York: Macmillan, 1960.

Randall, John H. "Substance as Process." *Review of Metaphysics* 10 (June 1957): 580–601.

Rist, John M. *Real Ethics.* Cambridge: Cambridge University Press, 2002.

Robinson, Daniel. *Aristotle's Psychology.* New York: Columbia University Press, 1989.

Ross, W. D. *Aristotle: A Complete Exposition of His Works and Thought.* Cleveland: Meridian, 1959.

Royce, Josiah. *The Religious Aspect of Philosophy*. New York: Houghton Mifflin, 1885.

———. *The World and the Individual*. Gloucester, Mass.: Peter Smith, 1889–1901.

Saliba, George. *Islamic Science and the Making of the European Renaissance*. Cambridge, Mass.: MIT Press, 2007.

Santayana, George. *Scepticism and Animal Faith*. New York: Dover, 1980.

Schlick, Moritz. *Philosophical Papers*. Translated by Peter Heath, et al. Edited by H. Muller and B. Van de Velde-Schlick. 2 vols. Dordrecht: D. Reidel, 1979.

Schmitt, Charles B. *Aristotle and the Renaissance*. Cambridge, Mass.: Harvard University Press, 1983.

Secada, Jorge. *Cartesian Metaphysics: The Scholastic Origins of Modern Philosophy*. Cambridge: Cambridge University Press, 2000.

Sharkey, Sarah Borden. *Thine Own Self: Individuality in Edith Stein's Later Writings*. Washington, D.C.: The Catholic University of America Press, 2010.

Sokolowski, Robert. *Husserlian Meditations: How Words Present Things*. Evanston, Ill.: Northwestern University Press, 1974.

Stein, Edith. *Finite and Eternal Being*. Translated by Kurt F. Reinhardt. Washington, D.C.: The Catholic University of America Press, 2010.

Strauss, David Friedrich. *Das Leben Jesu, 1835*. Translated by Peter C. Hodgson and George Eliot. Philadelphia: Fortress, 1972.

Thorndike, Lynn. *A History of Magic and Experimental Science*. 8 vols. New York: Columbia University Press, 1923–58.

Veatch, Henry. *Aristotle: A Contemporary Appreciation*. Bloomington, Ind.: Indiana University Press, 1974.

———. "Telos and Teleology in Aristotelian Ethics." In *Studies in Aristotle*, edited by Dominic O'Meara, 279–96. Washington, D.C. The Catholic University of America Press, 1974.

Von Mises, Ludwig. "Economic Calculation in the Socialist Commonwealth." In *Collectivist Economic Planning*, edited by F.A. Hayek. London: Routledge, 1935.

Wallace, William A. "Philosophical Setting of Medieval Science." In *Science in the Middle Ages*, edited by David C. Lindberg, 105–6. Chicago: University of Chicago Press, 1978.

———. *The Modeling of Nature: The Philosophy of Science and the Philosophy* of *Nature in Synthesis*. Washington, D.C.: The Catholic University of America Press, 1996.

White, Lynn, Jr. "Technology and Invention in the Middle Ages." *Speculum* 15 (1940): 144–56.

———. "The Dynamo and the Virgin Reconsidered." *American Scholar* 27 (1958): 183–94.

———, ed. *Frontiers of Knowledge in the Study of Man*. New York: Greenwood, 1969.

Whitehead, Alfred North. *Science and the Modern World*. New York: Macmillan, 1925. Fourth edition, New York: Mentor, 1953.

Wippel, John F. "Thomas Aquinas and the Condemnation of 1277." *Modern Schoolman* 72 (1995): 233–72.

———. "The Condemnations of 1270 and 1277 in Paris." *Journal of Medieval and Renaissance Studies* 7 (1977): 169–201.

Witt, Charlotte. *Substance and Essence in Aristotle*. Ithaca, N.Y.: Cornell University Press, 1989.

Wolpert, L. *The Unnatural Nature of Science*. Cambridge, Mass.: Harvard University Press, 1993.

INDEX

The Nature of Scientific Explanation was designed in Garamond Premier Pro and typeset by Kachergis Book Design of Pittsboro, North Carolina. It was printed on 55-pound Natures Recycled and bound by Sheridan Books of Ann Arbor, Michigan.